COLLATERAL KINDNESS

THE TRUE STORY OF AN ARMY INTERROGATOR IN IRAQ

PAUL HOLTON

PLAIN SIGHT PUBLISHING
AN IMPRINT OF CEDAR FORT, INC.
SPRINGVILLE, UTAH

© 2013 Paul Holton

ISBN 13: 978-1-4621-1096-4

Published by Plain Sight Publishing, an imprint of Cedar Fort, Inc.
2373 W. 700 S., Springville, UT 84663
Distributed by Cedar Fort, Inc., www.cedarfort.com

LIBRARY OF CONGRESS CATALOGING-IN-PUBLICATION DATA
Holton, Paul, author.
  [Saving Babylon]
  Collateral kindness / Paul Holton.
    pages cm
  "Previously published in 2005 by Perihelion Press"--Information from the publisher.
  ISBN 978-1-4621-1096-4 (alk. paper)
  1. Iraq War, 2003-2011--Personal narratives, American. 2. Soldiers--Utah--Biography. 3. Utah National Guard--Biography. I. Title.

  DS79.76.H655 2012
  956.7044'342--dc23
  [B]

                              2012041560

Cover design by Angela D. Olsen
Cover design © 2013 by Lyle Mortimer
Edited and typeset by Michelle Stoll

Printed in the United States of America

10 9 8 7 6 5 4 3 2 1

I dedicate this book to my loving wife and kids, who have supported me throughout my 42 years of military service and during my three deployments to Iraq. My wife took charge of everything during my absence and sacrificed much.

CONTENTS

INTRODUCTION

When I joined the Army National Guard as a scared eighteen-year-old kid in 1970, I hoped my enlistment might spare me from going to Vietnam. It did.

Who would have guessed that six years later I'd re-enlist. Patriotic passion was pumping in my veins; a sense of military mission had seeped into my pores. I started out as a boy unsure of my duty, but I grew into a man driven by duty. Duty to God. Duty to comrades. Duty to country.

When I was thrust into the midst of Desert Storm in 1991, I fully believed my role as a citizen-soldier would help re-establish the freedom and peace of the Kuwaiti people after a brutal invasion by a maniacal dictator-neighbor. I did more than that. As my wartime experience unfolded, I saw that my contribution made a difference to individuals, to a nation, and to the world community.

My first deployment to the Middle East introduced me to the scorching desert, Saddam Hussein, scorpions in my boots, blistering sandstorms, and inedible MREs. But it did not prepare me for Iraq.

I am continually asked by the curious and inquisitive, "So, what was it really like in Iraq?" My answer: My experience in Iraq was magical.

As they try to conceal a look of perplexed disbelief, I can only imagine what they are thinking: "C'mon. Iraq is a hellhole. It's nothing but sweltering heat, endless sand, and crazed extremists whose life ambition is to kill Americans as they blow themselves up."

In the midst of that war-torn inferno they saw on the news every night, I found a spiritual oasis. As enemy mortars shattered nearby hotel walls, Black Hawks thundered overhead, and the crackle of small arms split the night, I discovered a way to carve out some sacred space, a process that changed both Iraq and me forever.

The journey was totally unexpected—oh, I knew I was headed for a war zone. I had done that before. But how could I have known that I would end up close friends with several Iraqi generals? How could I have predicted I would fall in love with Iraqi children? And how could I have known my entire future would be determined by a single phone call?

Although the spiritual terrain I traversed was rugged and bleak, my ultimate destination was the oasis I sought. As an Army interrogator, my job was to get inside the heads of Iraqis. The oasis appeared as I looked into their hearts.

There is significant history being forged in Iraq right now. Democracy has been launched. Businesses are opening doors. Capitalism is creating opportunities. Alliances are being formed. Freedom is being tested.

It may be years before this history is taught to children in our schools. This historic saga is unfolding daily as American soldiers bear the torch of freedom to a part of the world where freedom's light has been in short supply. It changed my life to see what a glimmer of light can do for a nation that has struggled in darkness for decades.

Iraqis went out of their way to express appreciation for the work of the Coalition. Iraqi freedom was bought at a high price—American soldiers' blood. The Iraqis know it. And they aren't afraid to acknowledge it. *Collateral Kindness* is a glimpse into the history of Operation Iraqi Freedom that the American public needs to know.

In 1776, when the Declaration of Independence was first read in public and the Liberty Bell rang out in celebration, one witness said of that famous bell, "It rang as if it meant something." Freedom still means something.

I am continually thankful for the opportunity I had to work side by side with the Iraqi people, watching them discover that freedom has enduring meaning.

CHAPTER ONE

HOMECOMING 2004

A s the C-135s touched down in Salt Lake City, joy washed over me like a tidal wave. I looked out the plane's only window to see hundreds of people inside the National Guard hangar holding banners. Once on the ground, I walked down the tarmac toward the cheering crowd, where a small group of people holding a poster and a flag came running in my direction screaming, "Wiggles! Wiggles!" My family and a few close friends had broken past the barriers. I embraced them all, especially glad to see my son Michael, who had been serving in Russia for the past two years as a missionary for The Church of Jesus Christ of Latter-day Saints. It was complete joy knowing I was home, back among loved ones and back on American soil. I also realized that readjusting to life at home would take some time after the life-altering year I'd just survived in Iraq.

Later that February day, I sat in my kitchen gazing out through a fog-framed window watching giant snowflakes fall aimlessly, bending pine boughs and leaving the neighborhood swathed in a foot of white powder. The empty dog cage was covered with snow, causing me to reflect back on a time gone by when my dog, Jasmine, was still alive. I remembered playful times when we used to run around the yard together. I missed the past, was grateful for the present, and had great aspirations for the future.

My joy was short lived when, after only four days, I received a call informing me that I would be returning to Iraq immediately to take care of a few remaining issues relating to my investigation. The Army had not yet decided what they wanted to do with me, but requested me to be present in Baghdad in order to make a decision.

They expected me to be in Baghdad for about a month. I was not angry about going back to Iraq. Of course, I had no choice. But I also knew that the course of my life was in the Master's hands.

With the sound of the airplane engines gently humming in the background, lulling the passengers to sleep, I sat restlessly in my airplane seat trying to sort my mixed emotions on my way back to Baghdad. I was the only one from my unit returning to Iraq, so I figured this trip would be very different from the last one. I was promised it would be short, but not necessarily sweet.

My transatlantic flight sent me first to Amsterdam, and from there onward to Kuwait City. About thirty minutes after leaving Atlanta, just after jutting out over the Atlantic, one of the flight attendants came down the aisle with a faxed message from Colonel Long. His short message shook me to the core:

"Chief Holton: There has been a change in your mission. Do not proceed to Kuwait. Get off in Amsterdam. Return and go home."

I was not needed in Baghdad after all. This sudden turn of events was music to my ears and an answer to many prayers. Officers in my direct chain of command and General Tarbet, the two-star Adjutant General for the Utah National Guard, had all been working tirelessly to influence a decision before I was forced to return to Iraq, so I found it a bit ironic that the decision finally came down while I was 32,000 feet over the Atlantic. I was to be attached to my unit in Salt Lake City until they determined if I was needed back in Iraq.

This sudden turn in events was just the last in a long line of anxious days. I'd been cut off from my team, spent weeks waiting without word of when I would be returning to duty or going home, and finally found myself the subject of a military investigation. The cause of it all? For that, I have to go all the way back to the beginning, back to Iraq, back to the conception of my desire to make a difference in the lives of the people I saw suffering all around me.

Looking back, I realized then as now that all I could do was put my faith in God with a firm belief that I was in good hands. I trusted that things would work out the way He wanted them to in the end. At every moment, I knew the road ahead was going to be full of challenges and surprises, just like the road behind me, and would affect many more lives than just my own. Spending thirteen months

in a war zone—surrounded by death, destruction, and damage—
can deeply and irreversibly change a person. But I had survived, and
more: I had made a difference by focusing on the simple, the good,
the small acts of kindness.

To my own surprise, this experience placed me on an unexpected path. Through simple acts of love and kindness, I became
the founder of an organization called Operation Give, inadvertently
created by a desire to help others. Initially created to bring small
comforts to the Iraqi people, Operation Give has since exceeded all
expectation. Operation Give, armed with a simple but powerful mission, continues to propel me and my devoted team forward down
a road of small miracles, a road where anything is possible. Today,
Operation Give has a broader scope and vision, aiming to offer hope
and provide solutions to the deprived and disconnected people of the
world, determined to win hearts and minds and, perhaps, change
the perception of future generations. To this end, Operation Give
provides material supplies and resources to US Military men and
women stationed throughout the world, so they in turn can distribute these items to the people with whom they come in contact.

The story of this remarkable organization is also my story, born
in a harsh land of death and blood and proof that, no matter the
horrors that surround us, the choice of how we will govern ourselves
remains within each one of us.

CHAPTER TWO

A JOURNEY BEGINS

Are we going? Am I on the list?" I asked yet again.

It was just before Christmas 2002, and I could tell by his voice that Sgt. Jensen was getting perturbed with my calls. I couldn't blame him. Like many reservists, I had been contacting the National Guard Armory every day to discover my deployment status.

Tensions in the Middle East were escalating, and Saddam Hussein was becoming increasingly belligerent and uncooperative. Military action seemed unavoidable, so most of us in our Military Intelligence (MI) unit fully expected the phone call notifying us of mobilization.

"It's time," said the voice on the phone. "Be ready to move out on the seventh."

Along with the other one hundred and fifty Utah Army National Guardsmen, who were all part of a Military Intelligence Battalion, I was about to be launched on an unknown mission to an unfamiliar country for an undetermined period of time. I had only four days to prepare. Just four days to tie up loose ends at work and at home, pack my essential items, and prepare my family for an extended period of time without me. One day was consumed by the Soldier Readiness Process (SRP), a battery of pre-departure medical, dental, and vision exams to ensure medical readiness. The slug of immunizations and the distribution of medications, antidotes, and mask inserts let me know the nature of the risks awaiting me.

Preparing for deployment was not a new experience for me, having gone through it a decade before during Desert Storm. I knew what to expect each step of the way, recalling with precise detail the mobilization process, which would take me again to a Middle East desert with camels, veiled women, scorpions, sandstorms, and heat.

For four days, I dashed about as if my life depended on it—and it did—trying to make sure nothing had been forgotten, that family and work issues were settled, and that every possible needed item was packed. Once my mobilization files were in order and personal situations were handled the best they could be, I was ready to leave.

As usual, I packed heavy, going way over limit. If the limit was two boxes, I had four; I knew what I was going to need. I prepared for the worst and hoped for the best.

As I did during Desert Storm, I brought everything I would need to set up my kitchen with all the "fixin's," remembering all too well the awful taste and smell of a daily diet of MREs (meals, ready to eat). My enhancements made MREs ready to enjoy rather than ready to endure.

February 7, 2003, was an especially cold winter day, as we converged at Camp Williams, south of Salt Lake City. As I pulled into the parking lot, a large crowd of people had already formed to support my unit's departure for what was being referred to as an extension of Operation Enduring Freedom, America's war against terror in Afghanistan and elsewhere. The buses were lined up in front of the armory, and friends and family members were milling about like restless cattle before a thunderstorm.

With the help of my sons, I grabbed my bags and ventured over to the buses to load up my gear, but I was repeatedly stopped by numerous friends who had come out to see me off. With hardly a word being spoken, we embraced, knowing full well what might be in store for us in the days ahead. As I glanced over the crowd, I noticed old military buddies that I had served with in years past as well as some fellow tent-mates from the sands of Desert Storm. They were all there to show their support for those of us departing for this new conflict in the Middle East.

I embraced General Tarbet, Adjutant General for the Utah National Guard, who had initiated the call-up. He was the same individual who had called me to the Middle East some twelve years before. Now, with tears in his eyes, he wished me well.

"Good luck, Chief. Wish I could go with you." He echoed the

sentiments of others staying behind. "Make sure they all come back alive," he demanded. "And make sure they all keep their head in the game," he ordered, knowing precisely what would be required of us.

I made the rounds to ensure I expressed appreciation to all who had ventured out on a cold February morning, visiting with some I hadn't seen in years. Some were surprised to see me still in uniform departing for yet another life-changing deployment to the Middle East.

"I didn't know you were still in," some said. Those who knew me well knew I would make the most of it. "Glad you are going with them," some expressed. "It will be good to have a few older birds going with the young ones, not yet tempered by the winds of war," one old comrade commented.

My family had not prepared well for the bitter chill of the winter air; my daughter clung to those around her just to stay warm. It was all too familiar. I still had vivid memories of her and the other children clinging to my wife years ago as I drove away on a bus on a cold winter's day, heading off to Desert Storm. Suddenly, I found myself inching onto the bus.

"Good-bye. I love you, Dad." One by one, my kids waved their final farewells. There came a point where I couldn't look back anymore.

"Be safe," was chanted over and over again by all those who were standing near the bus. The diesel engines churned out pungent fumes as weeping family members backed away.

Before I knew it, the bus pulled out. The journey had begun, and I was now with my new family—my brothers and sisters of the military. The departure was emotionally afflicting, but my mind was already focused on the serious nature of our mission and the business at hand.

It was a physically and emotionally uncomfortable bus ride to Fort Carson in Colorado Springs, Colorado. Most were still in silent shock over what had just happened. I started a lighthearted movie in the bus to distract us from the images of our sad and crying loved ones, images that were still painfully fresh. I did everything possible to keep things loose and jovial.

* * *

We were an exceptional bunch of guys compared to typical Reserve units. Most had traveled extensively, and many had served as missionaries in various places around the globe. Most were spiritually oriented, with deep roots in faith and family. Our departure from the comforts of civilian life to an unfamiliar and threatening war zone had motivated many to become even more spiritual. As the bus pulled us away from the familiar surroundings of home, our mood was somber but our spirits were high. We were doing all we could to stay positive as we made the best of the situation.

Long bus rides lend themselves to introspection. I found myself pondering my leadership role in what our unit was about to experience. This was one of those times in life when no matter what happened, I was committed to maintaining a positive attitude and making the most of every situation. In my position as morale officer and chief warrant officer (CW4) and with so many young faces on board, I felt like everyone's father figure. I suspect my graying hair helped solidify that role. Here was an opportunity to be a positive force for change and development in these young soldiers' lives. I silently wondered if the key to success would be improving myself.

Deployment required all of us to be more considerate and more patient with each other. Even though we had not left the United States yet, tensions rose and many became increasingly frustrated with their new life. What might have been a minor social faux pas back home could blow up into a major crisis in this social pressure cooker. It was a difficult situation for many, testing their ability to adapt to the demands of a new life under new and unfamiliar circumstances.

* * *

After three weeks at Fort Carson, preparing to become soldiers of war, my unit finally got the call to move out. The message informed us that we would be leaving bright and early Monday morning at "0-dark-hundred." Our commander decided to give us some time off to spend our last stateside weekend with our wives, who had driven hundreds of icy miles to Fort Carson for a final farewell weekend.

"Go do whatever you want. Enjoy yourselves. But be back at the barracks Sunday evening at 1700," the commander ordered. "Say your good-byes and be ready to move out with all of your gear on the bus by that time." He made it crystal clear that we had to be ready to leave.

Leaving Fort Carson

I had a great weekend with my wife, spending a couple of nights in a nice hotel, indulging in the local cuisine of Colorado Springs, and just being together. However, always close to the surface was one surreal thought: "Before I know it, I will be in Iraq fighting a war."

In the final hours before departure, I couldn't escape thoughts of what I was facing. As a means of pointing that emotional energy in the right direction, I engaged my mind in a pep talk with myself:

"I believe in this important mission. Someone has to pay the price for freedom. My efforts will help create a land of freedom and democracy. I have skills that are needed, backed by years of experience, which I can share with others younger than I, who have been called upon for the first time to serve their country and the cause of freedom. I know that what I am doing is important for America, the Iraqi people, and the world. We are about to make history, changing the world forever by removing a tyrant from power. I am ready for whatever is to come, with no fear and no worries. My heart and mind are at peace."

We flew to the Middle East in a large chartered commercial jet, making several stops along the way. Each stop involved hours of waiting. I took every opportunity to keep the atmosphere light and in high spirits. At one time, after joking around with the crew, I was made an honorary flight attendant, pinned and everything. I was in charge of speaking to my troops on the plane over the intercom system, which gave me a chance to really cut up and interject some levity into an otherwise tedious trip.

* * *

We landed in Kuwait City around ten o'clock at night. It was the blackest night I'd ever seen. We were rushed onto several waiting buses—with curtains drawn for security—for transport to Camp Wolf, a stone's throw from the landing field.

"MOVE OUT! Quickly, quickly!" the instructions were snapped. "This is not a secured area," claimed the sergeant in charge. Of course that made us feel right at home. "Keep the curtains closed," was the command. This was the Army. This was war.

Next came the bus ride from Camp Wolf to Camp Udairi, which was something right out of *Raiders of the Lost Ark*. I had never been on such a long and bumpy bus ride in my life. It took almost three hours to get to the base on a two-lane road through the desert. Actually, there were no lanes, just people driving across the sun-baked desert sands in self-proclaimed lanes, the paved road having ended a short time after our departure.

We were jammed into small Kuwaiti buses with tiny uncomfortable seats. Our Indian drivers acted like this was some camel race to see who could get there first. We could barely fit half a butt cheek on the seat with two guys per seat. I was catching air off every bump, while our driver ignored all potential road hazards, perhaps to win the undisclosed prize at the finish line. To make the ride even more uncomfortable, the packs on our backs forced us forward on the seat. I was loaded down with all my military gear, including at least sixty pounds of essential equipment that I wouldn't go anywhere without:

gas mask, M16 rifle, Kevlar helmet, flak jacket, and chemical suit. But no complaints—I had been issued all this stuff because someone knew I would need it.

As we sped into the desert horizon, we continued on past several other US military bases along the way. I noticed that other bases were named after familiar places in the States, like Camp New York and Camp Virginia. It was comforting to see words and names I recognized as we sped to our base in the middle of nowhere. Of course, I couldn't help but wonder what *Udairi* meant—possibly an Arabic term for uninhabitable.

Arriving at the base late that night, our check-in took place in the pitch-blackness of the desert evening. I stumbled around trying to identify my bags from the rest that were strewn on the ground, after which I was directed to find my way in the unfamiliar darkness to the mess tent. Dinner ended up being two deep-fried chicken patties and some rice. After much difficulty, I figured out which tent I was supposed to be in, which surprisingly hadn't been arranged ahead of time. It was almost as if they weren't expecting the arrival of over a hundred soldiers. I threw my bags in the tent, set up my cot, and crashed on the spot. Gratefully, I slipped into an instantly sound sleep, a deserved reward for the ordeal I had just been through.

* * *

At Camp Udairi, I was living in a large Bedouin-style tent with about fifty other guys. The tent was just like the ones the desert tribes live in; well-designed for the desert environment, but not too spacious. Our personal space consisted of an area about six feet wide and six feet long, half of which was taken by the cot. The space around my cot provided room to hang things up and still left a small amount of space for my duffle bags and large black boxes. It wasn't easy to settle into that kind of cramped existence, but I didn't expect to be there too long. Mostly I hesitated to take out much of my stuff due to the ever-present Sand Monster.

In this pre-battle environment, the enemy was sand. I tried to maintain my positive energy, but it was hard to even function with sand blowing everywhere. Our moods went up and down with the

Our tents in Camp Udari

surging tide of sand-laden wind, known as *habood* in Arabic. For the first week, it was oppressively dusty with inescapable sandstorms all day, every day. It is difficult to imagine what these storms are like without experiencing one. The sand blended so fully with the air that I couldn't see in front of my face even inside my tent. It was impossible to keep the grit from invading everything—my weapon, my bags, my tent, my food. At times, breathing became a laborious process; with every breath, I sucked in sand like a giant vacuum. It sometimes felt like my lungs were filling up with dirt. I wished I had a dipstick to give me an accurate reading of my sand level.

In my twelve-year absence from the desert, I had forgotten how the desert wind blows, throwing its weight around and sandblasting your face with an abrasive furor. The particles were extremely fine, almost microscopic, creeping into every unsealed crack and crevice, making my ears and nose easy targets. I remember having to deal with the sand the last time I was in Kuwait, but you never get used to it. I hoped everyday that the wind would stop blowing or at least slow down long enough to make sight a possibility.

When it was time to eat dinner, all of us were required to suit up in full "battle rattle"—Kevlar helmet, bulletproof vest, and loaded weapon. I put a scarf around my face so I could breathe without inhaling a suffocating amount of sand. Having grown up around the

Great Basin in the western United States, I thought I was adapted to desert life—but not that desert. That place was a pit. I just couldn't imagine why anyone would choose to live there, even the tribal Bedouins who had lived there for centuries. My only temporary consolation was that in spite of the omnipresent sand, the temperatures were still below 100 degrees. But I knew the soul-scorching heat was coming soon.

One night, while a group of us were trying to get back from the mess tent with a plate of food in our hands, we encountered a sandstorm that suddenly blew in out of nowhere. The sand made it impossible to see anything in front of us and caused us to become completely disoriented. Like blind sheep, we repeatedly stumbled into barbed wire and other hidden road hazards in the darkness of the sand-filled night. We finally ran into someone with a light who knew the way back to our tents. We felt totally helpless against Mother Nature and her ferocity. The food we were carrying had been abundantly peppered with a layer of inedible grit.

* * *

As the sandstorms subsided, simple pleasures like walking outside and taking a deep breath were no longer unthinkable. When the sand wasn't blowing, there were moments when I was captivated by the bare beauty and timeless majesty of the desert. On a clear day you really could see forever. The sprawling sky took on a royal hue and the sunsets were extraordinary.

* * *

Camp Udairi housed over nine thousand soldiers in the weeks and days leading up to the war. The troop build-up made for long food lines and a shortage of many essentials, especially toilet paper. Bathroom issues, though never pleasant to think about, really had a significant impact on morale. One camp rule I never broke was to avoid the porta-potty during the hottest part of the afternoon. There were days that the outside air temperature climbed to 120 degrees and the latrines were probably over 140 degrees. An oven like that squeezed every last drop of perspiration out of you while burning your lungs with the most putrid steam imaginable. Out motto went something like this:

> To live to go another day,
> Never go in the heat of the day.

Our location was about twenty miles southeast of the Iraqi border. We knew the plan was to move into Iraq soon. The war plans were aggressive, with everyone expecting things to unfold quickly. Everything was pointing toward the war kicking off soon, within days. With our strategic position so close to the Iraqi border, our plan was to move north as fast as possible and to see Coalition troops eventually secure Baghdad.

I had been reading a number of books while at Udairi, which helped me understand the context and purpose of our mission. I knew that some of the people back home didn't understand or didn't agree with the war, but it was the only way to free these people from a dangerous, merciless, and ruthless leader. Saddam Hussein had killed thousands of his own people and would not hesitate to give his weapons of mass destruction to a terrorist organization or to use them himself, which he had done in the past.

After a week or so of doing nothing, I received my new assignment and a briefing on what our plans for action would be once the war started. I was assigned to work in the Battalion Tactical Operation Center (TOC), which was over Company A, where most of our people were assigned. My task was to manage the flow of reports and information that came in from the interrogation teams in the field and to publish those through all intelligence channels.

As real intelligence responsibilities began to materialize—coding documents, interrogating captives, deciphering messages—we knew that we were going to have to get reliable assistance from our Arabic-speaking interpreters that could be trusted. Locating, hiring, and training Arabic translators was essential to successful intelligence gathering.

Meeting the Iraqi civilian interpreters from the United States, almost twenty of them, was encouraging. They seemed intelligent, educated, and anxious to participate. They were hired to assist our group of interrogators in conducting interrogations in Arabic. My discussions with the interpreters were not only fascinating, but they also confirmed what I had read and heard about the situation in Iraq. All the interpreters were anxious for us to go north and take out Saddam's government, freeing the Iraqi people from the "wicked regime," as they put it. They made it evident that the Iraqi people had suffered greatly under Saddam's rule.

The accounts that the Iraqi interpreters related to me were both astounding and shocking. Our discussions revealed unthinkable atrocities Saddam had committed against his own people. He had been killing and torturing using gas and chemical weapons repeatedly throughout the last twenty years, either on the neighboring Iranians or the Kurdish minority within Iraq. Everyone knew he had weapons of mass destruction, and past experience had shown he would not hesitate to use them.

In our initial meetings, I tried to build a relationship with the interpreters, in hopes that I would become familiar with each of them personally before being thrust into an interrogation together. I needed to know, to some degree, each individual's personality, prejudices, and thinking process, which could interfere with or support my interrogation methods. Also, for more selfish reasons, befriending them would provide a means to get real food once a week when they were able to leave for Kuwait City on a weekly shopping spree. Fresh vegetables and fruits were like gold around camp—ingredients totally absent from our daily diet. I wanted to try some local cuisine, too, if I had the chance. Bring on the hummus and flatbread!

CHAPTER THREE

SHOCK AND AWE

On Tuesday, March 18, we woke up to the news that President Bush had given Saddam and his sons forty-eight hours to give up power and go into exile or face invasion by more than a 100,000 Coalition troops poised on Iraq's borders. "Their refusal to do so," said the President, "will result in military conflict commenced at a time of our choosing." We had spent nearly two months actively preparing for this exact moment. But the President's declaration that "all the decades of deceit and cruelty have now reached an end" let the men and women of the military know that our job was about to begin.

By the morning of Thursday, March 20, with less than eighteen hours remaining on Saddam's forty-eight-hour ultimatum, we were playing our own version of beach volleyball when we learned that President Bush would be giving an address to the American people. We immediately stopped our game to hear what the President had to say:

"On my orders, Coalition forces have begun striking selected targets of military importance to undermine Saddam Hussein's ability to wage war." Then speaking to the United States military personnel in the Middle East, the President continued with solemn resolve: "The peace of a troubled world and the hopes of an oppressed people now depend on you. That trust is well placed." The words of the President connected with the conviction of every soldier present at Camp Udairi that morning: "This will not be a campaign of half measures, and we will accept no outcome but victory. . . . We will bring freedom to others, and we will prevail."

In an address that lasted only four minutes, the President launched the war ahead of schedule—at least ahead of our schedule, surprising even our leaders. Everyone had expected the war to kick off in the evening, the trump card being our superior night-fighting capabilities, so it came as somewhat of a surprise that the war started during early morning daylight hours. But the timing made sense given the nature of the targets, and in spite of the surprise, we were ready. Even before the President's speech was over, reports of Tomahawk cruise missiles being launched towards Baghdad were streaming in. We learned later that air raid sirens, flashes of light, and US warplanes had decorated the early morning skies of Baghdad starting at 6:34 AM. Coalition aircraft would instantly bomb military targets to soften up the country's defenses against a broader air and ground attack. Instead of focusing on the demolition of Iraqi forces and factories, the objective would be to cripple the enemy's will to fight. An early-morning surprise attack with hundreds of smart bombs raining down on military and leadership targets would paralyze the country. Iraqi commanders would be cut off from their divisions. Forces in the field would be cowed by an enemy they couldn't see, and the Iraqi regime would assume early on that defeat was imminent and inevitable. This was the essence of our shock-and-awe strategy.

* * *

Later that evening, the kind of war we originally expected began. The sun set on Baghdad at 6:15 PM on March 20. At about 9:05 PM, US planes unleashed their muscle on military targets in central Baghdad. Explosions were reported close to the Royal Palace, the ministry of defense, and the Al-Rasheed Airport in the western part of the city. Within the first twenty-four hours of the war, US forces planned to light up Iraq with more than 1,500 bombs and missiles.

By 11:00 that evening, damage assessments were starting to pour in. One of Saddam's palaces had been destroyed. A residential compound in Baghdad where Saddam, his sons, and other key leaders may have been hiding was hit. An intelligence service headquarters and a Republican Guard facility had been severely hit. Heavy bombing also hit Tikrit, Saddam's family home, as well as the cities of Mosul and Kirkuk in the north.

The enemy was particularly busy the first night, launching missiles every hour all night long. Not all of them were Scuds, but unless we knew otherwise, we all reacted as if they were. The Scud missile is a Russian-made, surface-to-surface missile system with a range of about 300 miles. The most threatening aspect of a Scud is its unpredictability. The warhead can be explosive, chemical, or nuclear, and they have notoriously poor accuracy as they coast unguided to the target area. Camp Udairi was an airbase, with hundreds of helicopters of all sizes and shapes loaded down with all types of weaponry. It was quite a sight to see the Black Hawk and Apache helicopters positioned on the tarmac, ready for action. The Apache is the Army's attack helicopter complete with Hellfire missiles, rockets, and a 30mm chain gun. Its strong suit is versatility, as it delivers precision strikes in day, in night, and in adverse weather conditions. With a combat mission speed of 167 mph and a range of 300 miles, these helicopters—or "birds," as they are called—could be employed at a moment's notice around the clock. The Black Hawk is a utility tactical transport helicopter capable of transporting a fully equipped infantry squad faster and in a wider range of weather conditions than its UH-1 "Huey" predecessor.

Once the war started, our base was on alert for any Iraqi missiles launched in our direction. As soon as one was launched and the military knew the direction in which it was headed, an advance warning would go out to the entire Camp. We then had to jump into our chemical protective gear, run into a bunker, and wait for the "all clear" sound to go off. For the first few days of the war, we spent much of our time jumping in and out of bunkers and donning chemical protective suits, called MOPP gear. I considered moving my cot into the bunker so I wouldn't have to wake up, but it was my job to make sure that everyone was ready and that no one was having any problems getting their equipment on. Since we were never sure about the nature of the Scud missiles being launched in our direction, we took every precaution. Better safe than sorry.

Starting Thursday morning and continuing for the first few days of the war, Iraq was still capable of launching their Scud missiles against US troops in Kuwait. And given our position, size, and air-base status, I knew we were prime targets at Udairi.

Our star defender was the new Patriot surface-to-air guided missile defense system. Its Gulf War predecessor was designed to explode near slow-moving targets like aircraft, but was never intended to shoot down ballistic missiles. The new version of the Patriot is equipped with a hit-to-kill technology and is capable of intercepting Scuds at a higher altitude than was possible back in 1991. The interceptor would collide with the Iraqi missile like a bullet hitting a bullet. The exploding warhead is capable of destroying incoming Iraqi warheads, including any nuclear, chemical, or biological agents.

One evening, I was able to witness one of these Patriots in action. With batteries located on our base, about two hundred yards from my tent, I could hear the unmistakable sound of the Patriot's launch. I ran outside in my chemical suit and stared at the distant sky waiting for the hit. Instantly, a bright flash appeared, signaling that the Patriot had met its target. Seconds later, the sound of the collision could be heard, confirming success. We returned to our tents, resting a little more peacefully.

Our Patriot missiles went down on occasion while needed repairs were made. You can imagine my feelings one night when I got an email saying our base was not going to be protected by Patriots for a while. It was a good thing no one else knew about that, like the Iraqi Army. That would have ruined my day for sure.

* * *

In my responsibilities at the battalion's TOC, I made sure all of our teams got out on the right assignments and then assisted in managing the flow of intelligence and information from these teams. I was also assisting with arrangements to move the Joint Interrogation Facility (JIF) northward into Iraq when the time came. We recognized that the key to finding the "smoking guns," as the weapons of mass destruction were sometimes called, was intelligence gathering. To that end, we shouldered the responsibility for getting out accurate and timely reports to all of the intelligence channels and agencies.

As early as March 21, the second day of the war, a top Iraqi military commander along with his top deputy and thousands of troops, surrendered to US forces. On one of these early days of the war, a couple of Iraqi generals were captured, causing me to be busily engaged in lining up the interrogators to be flown to where the generals were being held.

Our group of MI soldiers was getting new missions daily as the need arose to question captured POWs. As various cities were taken by Coalition forces, many of the Iraqi commanders were surrendering, with their whole units capitulating.

With the word that several teams were leaving Camp Udairi in the morning, I hurried over to our tents to visit with fellow soldiers from my Utah unit and to say good-bye to those leaving on what was called Team Wheeler, a Mobile Interrogation Team (MIT). I gave them some last-minute advice and took a moment to have a team prayer. Five of them would be leaving in the morning to go to where several high-ranking Iraqi officers were being held by the Marines. They would be crossing the berm and traveling into the war zone, into an area that had just been taken by our rapidly advancing forces.

* * *

The first Sunday after the start of the war provided the opportunity to attend church for about an hour, which was just what I needed. It gave me and the other soldiers who went the chance to get our heads spiritually refocused. It was a welcome break to have time to meditate and pray. During the course of the church services, Sgt. Hodgson retold the story of *Saving Private Ryan*. The last words that Tom Hanks spoke to him before he died was "Earn it," which is what we all needed to be thinking about. Earn it. Be worthy of the blessings that we are asking for. Earn the respect of others around us. Earn the trust of our fellow soldiers, and earn the love of our families and fellow countrymen.

As I walked back to my tent following the services, I had much to reflect on. My feelings about the war began to take on a spiritual tone. I had a feeling I was part of a bigger plan, one that was divinely developed, one that had something to do with blessing the Iraqi people. My mind and heart were open to the promptings of the Spirit—the "still small voice" spoken of by Isaiah, the Old Testament prophet—which enabled me to comprehend the importance of our presence in Iraq and the seriousness of our mission.

It was about ten o'clock, and most everyone was already asleep, expecting another night of Scud alarms, which would probably keep me up all night. There were a few guys playing cards on a makeshift table, with their gas masks close by. The night air was unusually kind of cool; I wasn't sure why. The night sky had a unique haze, which created a strange ring around the moon just coming up above the horizon. It was extremely dark out, which caused me to think to myself that it would be good for the night raids that had been planned.

Most nights, I stayed up late reading and writing in my journal, getting to bed around midnight, and then immediately falling fast asleep. I generally slept soundly and peacefully in my desert tent, except for the interruptions of nightly Scud alerts. One night, out of curiosity, I went outside during one of the missile attacks. To my surprise, I was able to hear the sounds of artillery pounding away at Iraq and the sound of helicopters leaving to and returning from missions. In the distance, like an exploding star, I was even able to see one of the patriots intercept a scud missile, exploding in a flash of light that quickly vanished from my sight.

It was a strange feeling to be out in the desert late at night with a war going on all around me, knowing that people were dying and putting their lives in harms way. Peoples' lives were changing on both sides, and things would never be the same again. While I was standing there, I could feel the concussion of each artillery shell being fired, feeling the air move and the push of the explosion against my face. The dust was stirred up all night long as helicopters went to and from, going out on missions and returning. I prayed for those young men, who were risking their lives that night, entering into a variety of dangerous situations and returning to do it again another day.

In the days that followed, although the winds and sandstorms continued making life difficult for all of us, I had gotten used to them to some degree. I found that the best way to deal with them was to avoid them. So I tried to stay inside my work area, where it was somewhat dust-free. In the TOC, we had a special kind of tent equipped with its own filtration system. This kept us fairly well sealed off and kept out most of the dust and sand in order to protect the computers.

Although we had access to televised CNN and FOX News, along with BBC radio news, the best and most reliably informative part of my day was the morning briefing. Every day around sunrise, I could be found waiting for the morning briefing to begin. It was encouraging to receive these updates on what was happening in the war, and the news was generally very good.

On day two of the war, Coalition forces were already making impressive strides on the ground, traveling over one hundred miles into Iraq from our positions in Kuwait. Bradley Fighting Vehicles and Abrams tanks were rolling unimpeded toward Baghdad in a wave of steel nearly twenty miles long. By March 23, just four days into the war, we had secured several major cities and ports in the south.

Our forces were moving well and making good time as they approached Baghdad. The real trick was to keep our supply lines open and secured, allowing our support team to get supplies through to our advancing forces. One day we got word that a small unit was ambushed and a few people killed. That was disheartening. But overall the early days of the operation had been very successful with few Coalition casualties.

The news media made it sound like the military was getting bogged down, but that was definitely not the case. There was a lot the media didn't follow, didn't know, and didn't report, even with embedded reporters. All too often the media seemed to focus on the few incidents when things went wrong. But those were isolated and did not represent the totality of what was really happening. The war continued to progress as planned, with many operational and battlefield successes. With less than ten days of war under our belt, we had over 100,000 Coalition forces inside Iraq. That feat alone was evidence of phenomenal success.

There was an abundance of rumors and outright lies floating around that were snatched up by overzealous reporters looking for the "big story." I was generally skeptical and occasionally sickened by the way the media outlets were portraying the war. They had such a short-sighted view of things and the notion that it was all supposed to be played out in a few days. I suspect that this approach actually worked in our favor at times, knowing the enemy was also watching the news.

While standing in the line for chow one day, I was surprised to see FOX News reporter Geraldo Rivera. He was in line to get some of that good Army grub just like me, so I said "Hi" and talked to him for a few minutes. As usual, the line was moving slowly, enabling one of the soldiers to run back to his tent and bring back his camera before Geraldo got through the line. I took some pictures with him and chatted a bit about his purpose for being there. I told him I appreciated the fact that he was putting himself in harm's way to get the news and that his support for the troops really meant a lot. He smiled and nodded as he loaded his plate.

I relished my fleeting brush with celebrity, but as soon as I looked at what I was being fed, I was quickly thrust back into the reality of military life.

* * *

Reports from Iraqi POWs were starting to come in at an increasing rate. There were reports of captured documents, captured locations, and captured equipment—all of which pointed to our success. A great deal of valuable intelligence was being gathered, which helped greatly in winning the war and proving to the world what Saddam had been up to.

More and more information was flowing in about what the Iraqis were doing to their own people to force them to fight against the oncoming Coalition forces. Rumors were spreading about how the Iraqis had started shooting their own soldiers and even civilians on the spot if they wouldn't fight. I also heard stories of kidnappings in which children were abducted and their fathers coerced to fight in exchange for the child's release. I was deeply troubled by the way the Iraqis continued to use hospitals, churches, and mosques as fronts for their military operations.

Some Iraqi soldiers put on our uniforms to disguise themselves as Americans. They were able to initially fool some Coalition troops, getting close enough to begin firing on them and killing several. The next day, to disable that strategy, soldiers put on their rubberized desert-camouflage chemical pants to distinguish themselves from any Iraqi soldier masquerading as an American. There were also reports of Iraqi commanders shooting anyone who surrendered, in a desperate attempt to create fear and uncertainty in the minds of their soldiers.

One report from Marines stationed at a checkpoint near Najaf revealed the mind-set of the enemy and their disregard for human life. As an Iraqi van was moving through a Marine checkpoint, the Marines motioned to the van to stop several times, but the van just kept on moving through the checkpoint without making any effort to stop. The Marines had ample justification to shoot since, just two days earlier, five US soldiers were killed when a suicide bomber attacked a checkpoint in Najaf. Finally, having no other choice given the incidents of suicide bombings, the Marines opened fire on the van. As they approached the wreckage, the Marines discovered they had shot seven women and children hidden in the back. The Iraqi military had done this deliberately so they could broadcast to the world that Americans were killing innocent women and children. Iraqis had also been strapping women and children to the outside of vehicles in order to safely cross bridges and roads.

People that accused the US military of killing innocent women and children have no understanding of the extent to which we went to avoid such loss. The US military, at times to our own detriment, went out of our way to avoid the loss of innocent people—even when we knew the enemy would never use such measures to protect our civilians or even their own wives and children. Never in the history of the US military have we been so committed to minimizing collateral damage in all operations.

Every day, more intelligence on Saddam was surfacing. It confirmed what we had long heard about what a terrible tyrant he was. I was sickened by the stories of what he did to his own people, to the Kurdish people, and to our soldiers who were their POWs. These and other reports provided a stark contrast between the way we treated our POWs and the way they treated theirs. Even when considering the unfortunate events at the Abu Ghraib Prison, there remain striking and fundamental discrepancies between the two systems.

From my experiences of the past thirty-four years as an interrogator in the US Army, I can speak with substantial authority and firsthand experience about the measures taken by US military to ensure the well-being of our POWs. Part of our battle plan took into account our responsibility to clothe, feed, and provide necessary medical treatment for our POWs. We were all disturbed by the cruelty and inhumane practices conducted by the Iraqi military.

Based on all the intelligence that was being gathered, I was starting to get a real sense of what it must have been like to live under such a brutal dictator. It must have been terrifying to live with the constant fear that at any moment, for the slightest reason, you or someone in your family could be shot, kidnapped, imprisoned, or killed—and thousands were. Saddam had created an unbelievably elaborate system to ensure his own survival and longevity. He was obsessed with his own security, watching everyone and everything, with organizations to watch organizations and other organizations to watch them.

During these first two weeks of the war, I was working twelve-hour shifts processing incoming intelligence with no days off. In the face of this demanding schedule, I still took time to reflect upon my second mobilization to a war in the Middle East. Outside my tent, I could see the orange glow of burning oil wells tinting the evening sky. By day, the smoke and dark haze on the distant horizon hung as a reminder of a tyrant obsessed with maintaining his brutal grip on the resources and people of Iraq. I contemplated the value and scope of my contribution as an American soldier and citizen of the world and became increasingly aware that my personal effort and that of my unit was helping to save lives and shorten the length of this war.

This was not about us, but about the Iraqi people. Our success in this conflict would bring freedom to an oppressed nation. Iraqis had lived in fear for so many years that it had become a way of life for them. The silent majority had been forced into submission by the brutal extremes of a dictator bent on securing his tyrannical rule.

There is a price for freedom, known all too well by the men and women on the front lines who are willing to pay it. Death is expected as a part of this struggle. Lives have been lost here, but very few in comparison to other military actions around the world. Fortunately, the United States has the might, the technology, and the firepower to minimize the loss of lives on both sides. Every precautionary measure was taken to ensure that the fewest lives were lost on both sides.

But not all of the casualties of war were immediate deaths. I couldn't help but think about the children, neglected and largely forgotten in this struggle. What happens to children in this kind of setting and this kind of environment? What damage are we doing to them? And there were many others, ignored and disregarded individuals, who as a result of birth were not fortunate enough to be born into the "right" class. The Kuwaitis hired these kinds of people to perform all the manual labor in our compound, people from places like India, Nepal, and Bangladesh. The Kuwaitis generally treated these workers like second-class citizens, devoid of any perceived value. But the services they provided were, in my mind, invaluable. These workers were all over the camp, putting up tents, making and serving our food, and performing all kinds of odd jobs. On a daily basis they brought water to refill our water tanks and rode around on large poop trucks to clean out all of our porta-potties. With thousands of soldiers housed in my compound alone, they had a big job of it. I can't think of much worse than a full porta-potty when you need to sit down and take care of business.

During my stay, I tried to befriend as many of them as possible, frequently going out of my way to talk to them, a difficult feat due to the fact that most of them don't speak English. In my experience, the workers always seemed eager to interact with us, greeting me with big smiles. One day, in a stroke of luck I was able to round up a few eggs from the nearby city. I had brought a box of pancake mix from home, and with my find I was able to cook up a large batch of scrambled eggs and pancakes. What a treat! Everyone I was able to share it with immediately gobbled it down. For a moment we thought we were in heaven.

I had also developed strong friendships with our Iraqi linguists, many of whom had come from the States to serve as interpreters during the conflict. One of them in particular, Joseph, I found to be extremely friendly and hospitable. Every time I saw him, he would invite me into his tent, motioning for me to enter and sit on his cot, offering me something to eat or drink. Often, these invitations were extended after our weekly food deliveries from Kuwait City, and over time I came to know Joseph well. He was a Christian and had been living in Detroit for some time with his wife and kids. He was from the northern part of Iraq and told me a number of terrible stories relating to the persecutions they had endured at the hands of Saddam over the years, stories filled with the torture and deaths of many people he'd known. We had some great discussions about the situation in Iraq before the war, conversations that had a lasting impact on my desire to help others like him.

You see, as you have probably guessed by now, I have a strong love for America and for the principles it stands for. I also have a deep admiration for anyone who believes in the principles of freedom, equality, and righteousness. I am a member of The Church of Jesus Christ of Latter-day Saints, a "Mormon" (just for the record, no, Mormons don't have more than one wife and yes, we are Christians). I am very proud of my ancestors, pioneers who paid the ultimate price to exercise their right for the freedom of worship. Perhaps it was a part of the spirit of devotion to my country, or maybe the light of Christ in me, that first compelled me to address those I saw in need. The words of my own religious upbringing rang in my ears, reminding me that "the worth of a soul is great in the sight of God." I felt then, and feel now, that I was in Iraq for a divinely inspired reason, even if I did not know what that reason was at the time. I firmly believe that I can make a difference, one person at a time.

CHAPTER FOUR

TRAGEDY AND CHANGE

By April 1—just thirteen days into the war and sooner than expected—our forces reached the outskirts of Baghdad, nineteen miles from the center of the city. This progress pleased the war planners, I'm sure. But it also placed our troops inside the Red Zone where Saddam was most likely to use his chemical weapons. There would also be several days of waiting on the outskirts before launching the Battle of Baghdad. This gave us time to secure our ground positions and to batter Baghdad military and leadership targets with our air power.

On April 6, our forces had isolated Baghdad and closed off the major roads into the city. In a taunting display of military might, our tanks made a brief foray into a Baghdad suburb, crossing the city limits for the first time. To the south, Iraqi forces had lost control of Basra after columns of British troops poured into Iraq's second-largest city.

That night, after a long and tiring day, I had just laid my head on my pillow when I was awakened by my commander. Expecting news about the war, I was startled to hear him informing me that my mother had passed away unexpectedly in her sleep the previous night. I was so shocked to hear the news that I couldn't find the words to respond. I sat there stunned and speechless, a flood of emotions running through my heart. Most of all, I felt robbed that she had left before I could say one last good-bye. I was always close to my mother, a kind and gentle woman, and we continued to have a warm and loving relationship throughout my adult years. But death doesn't always give us a warning call or a heads-up before it strikes. The war reminded me of that daily.

On a satellite phone call that evening, I was able to speak with my sister about mom's passing and the immediate steps required of me for her funeral and other arrangements. My sister tried to coax me to stay in Iraq to finish my work there, promising she would take care of mother's affairs. She obviously understood me quite well, knowing my feelings about duty, responsibility, and honor. I wrestled with the decision to leave, but at the same time I knew I would not be able to stay in Iraq. My MI unit was ready to move north where the new focus of our work would take place. I desperately wanted to be a part of that new assignment. My impending departure would be an abrupt derailment of the mission I was there to perform. But the Army expected me, as they would any other soldier, to return home. I also felt a deep sense of responsibility to support my family at this time of great loss.

That night, sleep was neither a priority nor an option. As I sorted through my gear, my mind filled with thoughts of my mother and a lifetime of tender memories. I went outside for a moment and looked up into the desert sky with tear-filled eyes to express my love for her, knowing she would be listening. I wanted to be star-struck by the desert night one more time. Locking my sights on the Big Dipper, which in turn pointed to the North Star, my passion to go north to Baghdad was charged. By dawn I was packed and ready to go, impatiently waiting for the 10 a.m. convoy that would take me to Kuwait City. Despite my preoccupation with the return trip home, I was overwhelmed as my men and coworkers came out to say their good-byes, expressing their love and concern for me. Just before my departure, my commander, Major Price, took me aside and told me I was his strength and that he would miss me greatly. It was an emotional departure that lent me great comfort over the next three days of travel back to Salt Lake City. Strangely, I was already missing the sand-encrusted wasteland that was Iraq and the people I rubbed shoulders with on a daily basis. I agonized over the fact that our troops were poised on Baghdad's perimeter and I was not there to finish the fight. However, I consoled myself by pondering what Iraq and its people had taught me so far. I was a better person, viewing myself and my life's purpose differently. I appreciated the little things in life even more. I hoped to never forget the feelings, experiences, and memories washing over me as I returned home to my family.

* * *

My return to the States occurred just as the war effort was reaching a dramatic climax. With US forces driving north and encircling Baghdad, there had been many compelling stories of heroism, sacrifice, and concern for the Iraqi people. But I was still filled with apprehension and uncertainty, knowing that the looming Battle of Baghdad would bring different and unexpected challenges.

In the early days of the war, Mobile Interrogation Teams (MITs) and Mobile Exploitation Teams (METs) were sent up north for short periods of time on vital intelligence-gathering missions. We were facing a flood of information, which expanded daily. Ours was the daunting work of processing this data for the intelligence community.

Our intelligence work was like putting together a jigsaw puzzle. There were so many pieces of this puzzle, which seemed to be connecting in front of us as our troops moved toward Baghdad. Each new wave of incoming intelligence was like having another five-hundred-piece puzzle added to the mix of partially connected pieces. There was always more to connect to an ever-expanding puzzle.

It was mind-boggling to contemplate the amount of information that needed to be dug up and the sheer number of people that needed to be interrogated. As we interviewed people about what had been going on in Iraq, we were deluged with accounts of atrocities shared by Iraqi citizens now that the floodgates had finally been opened. Even at this early stage of the war, a clear picture was emerging of Saddam's reign of terror, which was marked by heartless brutality and genocidal outbursts. For me, I didn't really care if the weapons of mass destruction were ever found. Saddam was an international fugitive and a war criminal. Twenty-five years of Saddam's tyranny had torn apart a nation and disrupted the entire region.

Just before my departure, half of our MI unit moved north toward Baghdad as the advance party to prepare the site for the rest who would be joining them later. This advance party would be in Iraq for some time, gathering information and intelligence before the rest of our unit assembled at that advanced location.

For our unit, the waiting was over; our mission was now beginning. It was time for us to take center stage and do what we were sent

29

to do. I was mentally prepared to go the distance and committed to seeing this through. But as the jet toward home lifted off the runway leaving Kuwait in the distance, I felt the responsibility of unfinished business. By leaving before my mission was completed, it seemed I was breaking faith with my men and turning my back on what needed to be done to ensure their safe return.

* * *

It wasn't hard to reacquaint myself with the comforts of home life; I enjoyed them so much. I took special notice of simple things like a comfortable chair, hot water from the tap, and a thermostat to set my home temperature to whatever I wanted it to be. Americans live in such luxury and comfort compared to many places in the world.

As soothing as the comforts of home were, I couldn't escape the images of my life in a tent with all of the gear and equipment cramping my style and limiting my space. Clotheslines were strung throughout the tent, and we sat on handcrafted, makeshift furnishings. My individual space consisted of my cot, my cot-straddling shelf, and a small table at the end of the cot that extended out into the middle of the tent. I was able to sit on my cot and write or type on the table.

To the left of my cot I had put down a couple of prayer rugs to give my feet a soft resting place. Most of the time, I'd remove my boots and run around barefoot in the tent, enjoying the soft feeling of the rugs on the bottom of my feet. I had a small table wedged between my cot and the one next to mine. On the surface of this table I had drilled holes, into which a variety of cups could be placed—makeshift drink holders. My clothes were hung up behind me on the roping of the tent, each article hung inside a plastic bag to keep out the ever-encroaching sand. Each morning I folded up my bedding, placed it under the cot-straddling shelf, and draped a poncho over all my gear.

In Salt Lake City, even though I was at a comfortable and safe distance from my tent in Camp Udairi, I couldn't put those memories away. I had gone home to fulfill the needs of my family, to offer a eulogy at my mother's funeral, and to handle the many details following her death. The days that followed brought many difficult circumstances as well as some tender and trying times. It was right for me to be there.

* * *

Home time is different from Army time. Home has a more predictable, manageable pace, one with a fair amount of autonomy. Army life, on the other hand, is highly structured, but you spend much of the time in suspense. Then once something happens, you don't always understand the motive, rationale, or outcome. Waiting has always been a familiar feature of military life, which can lead to serious boredom.

Many of the soldiers in Kuwait had been there since November 2002, waiting for the war and their jobs to begin. The preparation and waiting time turned into days, weeks, and months of doing not much of anything. I saw soldiers react to boredom differently. In fact, how they used their free time was often a more telling test of character than any experiences on the front lines. The real character of a man seems to come out when he has nothing to do.

Some soldiers spent their time worrying about when they were going home or how long they were going to be there or what they were going to do tomorrow. They spent too much time discussing what every order meant, forever trying to figure out the underlying politics of any action and reading between the lines, as if they were going to discover some hidden meaning that might help them make sense of everything. That just doesn't happen in the Army.

There were also those that complained about everything. Being an "armchair general" made them feel superior to everyone else, however briefly. They continuously looked for ways to find fault with things, something easy to do in the Army.

I decided to take charge of my own environment and exert control over those things that were within my sphere of influence. I saw every experience as an opportunity. To make my stay in the Middle East worthwhile, I had to create my own opportunities. There was nothing to be gained by worrying, criticizing, or complaining. It was within my power to choose how to respond to any situation. I had the ability to select my direction and to choose my outcome. That had always been my approach while serving in the Army, and if I was to return, I expected to maintain that perspective.

Despite the uncertainty, I knew I had unfinished business in Iraq. There was still a mission at hand. And my desire to complete that mission with my men was still burning bright within me. I was repeatedly told by Major Price to do whatever it took to stay home, but I knew the Army better than that, and after only three weeks of civilian life, my orders came to return to Iraq.

By May 7, 2003, I was back in the sand. In my short absence there had been many changes. While I was gone, the toppling of Saddam had become quite literal as US Marines helped a crowd of Iraqis pull down a massive statue of the dictator in the heart of Baghdad. Widespread looting, lawlessness, and general chaos followed. Throughout the country, Iraqi Army divisions surrendered or instantly disbanded as US troops restored order to places like Tikrit, Mosul, and Kirkuk. Many of my good friends had moved on to other assignments, to fulfill other missions. It was strange to see the camp so empty, with almost everyone I knew gone. My unit had been spread out all over Iraq on a variety of missions. Those of us in MI had a mounting supply of work with the daily capture, defection, or surrender of generals, government ministers, Baath Party leaders, and other characters whose faces appeared on the deck of playing cards featuring our most-wanted suspects. The increasing heat was another major change. Many mornings, I was awakened abruptly by sweat running down the middle of my back and was surprised to see the temperature in the tent had already reached over 100 degrees.

And then there was the increasing insect population sharing our tent. The flying bugs were especially attracted to the light of my computer screen. They swarmed around my head as if at any moment they were going to launch their assault and take over my computer.

In the weeks after my return, I could see that the conditions of camp life and the war were starting to wear on people. The heat, the sand, the insects, the close quarters, the lack of amenities, the lack of creature comforts—it all started to affect people in different ways. As soldiers continued to wait in this harsh environment for their assignments, their true selves usually crept to the surface. Some spoke about suicide; others would just as soon kill someone else who was getting on their nerves. Some just couldn't stand it anymore and didn't know what to do; others got depressed or frustrated.

Me, I found relief through focusing on my purpose for being there in the first place. Our challenge in Iraq was to help free a people from a dictator and assist them in setting up a new government with a bunch of untested people, people without a strong democratic tradition. We wanted them to get off on the right foot now that Saddam was gone. We knew there were many different groups and factions, all with competing and conflicting interests. Everyone there seemed to have their own agenda, with an overriding desire to protect their own domain. We knew forging freedom in that environment would be difficult. But the magnitude of that mission enabled me and many other great soldiers to keep our heads in the game.

One of my friends gave me the following appropriate analogy of our time in Iraq. He recalled the main character in the movie *Dancing with Wolves*, Lieutenant Dunbar, played by Kevin Costner. You might recall that this soldier was sent out to man a post on what was then the American frontier, a post that turned out to be a tiny, deserted cabin in the middle of nowhere. Although he found evidence of others that had been there before him, the isolation and danger of this post had possibly driven them to abandon their duty.

The difference between Dunbar and his predecessors was simply that he decided to take charge of his own environment, to control the things that were within his personal sphere of influence. He did not spend time worrying over that which he could not change. He simply accepted the situation as it was and did his best to better it in as many ways as possible. Realizing that he was not alone on the prairie, he decided to make contact with the native peoples nearby. He was not told to do this; he had been given no instructions regarding what was expected of him. Instead, he exercised his own agency and abilities and, by doing so, created a number of opportunities.

It is interesting to note that Dunbar could have reacted to that environment in so many different ways. He could have been negative, complaining about how terrible things were. Or he could have given up entirely and returned to his home. But he chose to reach out, to make contact with the people, learning their culture and their language, recognizing the value in their culture and traditions and, in the end, meeting the love of his life. When my time comes to depart this life, I can think of no greater tribute than the one given by Dunbar's adopted tribe, a fierce warrior atop his proud steed, shouting to the world as if to say "my life will never be the same because of you."

* * *

When I returned to Iraq, it was nice to see that my men had saved my cot area and the cot furniture I had built. They even put my name up over my area and made sure no one messed with it. That was a very kind gesture, one that I will never forget. They were all anxious to see me—at least it seemed that way—and they were anxious to hear how going home was, launching a barrage of a million questions at me. It was a very warm welcome, one that helped me get readjusted to this place again quickly.

It was now May and extremely hot, as usual for that time of year—at 8 AM, the temperature in the tent had already reached over 100 degrees. It seemed as though the heat alone in the mornings worked like my personal alarm clock, letting me know it must be time to get up. (Fortunately it did cool off nicely in the evenings, down to a bearable temperature.) Of course it was not the middle of the summer yet, so it was too early to tell what the real summer was going to be like. I could hardly wait to experience the fullness of summer's wrath in this wasteland.

But it was the desert nights I loved most. Night offered a reprieve from the harshness and irritations of the day. In the darkness, it was unusually calm, with nothing more than a slight cooling breeze drifting across the desert floor. The calm and certain serenity beckoned me out of my tent to roam the sands, capturing a rare moment of peace. It was as if the desert was bipolar: normally a harsh place, unforgiving and unbearable during the daylight hours, yet it was still capable of winning your trust with its moments of calm, only to turn on you with its next hot breath of sand and wind. This daily unpredictability added a level of diversity that actually made the desert more interesting.

CHAPTER FIVE

A HOME CALLED BUCCA

When I finally got the call to leave Udairi, it was like an answer to prayer. I was instructed to report to Camp Bucca in southern Iraq near the port city of Umm Qasr, where I would be working directly with Iraqi POWs. Camp Bucca was a POW camp set up on a large plot of land, which would be the temporary home for several thousand Iraqi prisoners. The piece of property was virtually unused by the Iraqis before the war, except for the radio station and tower that sat right in the middle of it. Camp Bucca had become the prisoner of war camp for all military prisoners, especially those of high rank. Seventeen of these prisoners were generals, and many more were colonels in the Iraqi military, and while imprisoned there they were my responsibility.

In retrospect, Bucca, with all its heat, snakes, and sandstorms, became for me a key turning point in my deployment and a life-changing catalyst for everything that was to follow—and for what later became Operation Give. There were many external factors and divinely inspired forces that propelled me on to what has become my life's work. Due to the positive interactions I had with the Iraqi generals at Camp Bucca and the example set by those around me, my attitudes and feelings were permanently formed and cemented into my heart and mind. You see, the Iraqis' inherent goodness won my heart long before I was exposed to the coexisting dark side.

There were of course two sides to our world, as there are in most places, but never before so distinctly obvious as in Iraq. There was a good side, with good people who really did want Iraq to be free, with all the freedoms that we enjoy. There was also a bad side full of the most evil parts of society. There were many of my fellow soldiers in Baghdad who had a much different experience than I. The way our attitudes were formed was based on the type of interaction we had with the people we came in contact with.

On the one hand, organized crime took over the minute Baghdad fell. They were up and running in so many parts of that society, snatching up opportunities for murderously selfish personal gain. It amazed me to see all of the opposing organizations that existed, now fiercely jockeying for position and power. But on the other hand, it was far more encouraging for me to see the goodness demonstrated by Iraqis like my generals and colonels, those whom I had the good fortune of interrogating at Camp Bucca. Unexpectedly, I witnessed the way that kindness begets kindness, and I became convinced that such an approach is really the only way to win the hearts and minds of others. My later interactions with the generals' family members, especially their children, as well as my brief encounters with the children playing in the streets of Umm Qasr, further cemented my desire and resolve to do whatever I could to ease their pain and suffering.

* * *

Camp Bucca was named in honor of Fire Marshall Ronald Paul Bucca, who died on September 11, 2001, during the terrorist attacks on the World Trade Center in New York City. Radio transmissions revealed he had ascended to the seventy-eighth floor of one of the buildings and was putting water on a fire when he died. His body was found close to one of the stairwells on October 23, 2001. In addition to being a twenty-three-year veteran of the Fire Department of New York, Ronald Bucca was also a twenty-nine-year veteran of the military and held the rank of warrant officer in the US Army Reserve. Most of his career was with the 11th Special Forces Group and the Defense Intelligence Agency as an intelligence analyst.

Camp Bucca in its prior life was a propaganda radio station for Saddam Hussein. The huge radio antenna positioned in the center of the compound reached high into the clear Iraqi sky. Local villagers told us of the types of things that were broadcast during Saddam's reign, which included deliberate misinformation on the progress of

Coalition troops during the early days of the war. Major Price and I occupied the radio station buildings, set up our office and operation center, and made this our home.

In an effort to make it seem more homelike, I set up our clotheslines, laid out the prayer rugs, and neatly arranged our boxes around the room. But during the intense heat of mid-afternoon, which hovered around 120 degrees, our office was like an oven inside. The temperatures inside the tents were no better, easily climbing to 125 degrees. To escape the heat, several of us slept on the roof. Every night we climbed a ladder, bedding in hand, to sleep under the stars, where a cooling breeze made conditions a little more bearable and sleep a little more possible. There were six of us sleeping on the roof, while the rest were sleeping in the tents set up not too far away. Occasionally, when the wind picked up you could see our silhouettes scampering around, grabbing our stuff, and heading down the ladder to get out of the storm.

We had made a large cooler with pieces of Styrofoam found lying around. This makeshift ice chest was about three feet square and appropriately named the Mother of All Coolers. Amazingly, it really worked. Bags of ice could be kept in there for days. I thought that my next project would be to build the "cooler coffin," big enough to sleep in. That would have been the perfect camp bed, sleeping in a cooler on ice.

At its peak in May, there were over ten thousand prisoners at Camp Bucca, which was an unbelievable sight and created an indescribable stench. It's difficult to comprehend the mess that many people can create. In addition to the prisoners, there were thousands of US forces living in cramped quarters, with all of us using nothing more than a slit trench for a bathroom. Even after the prisoner population was reduced to about one thousand, there was still a stench about that place I will never forget.

Flies quickly became a serious problem. Millions of these pesky little insects would feast in the slit trenches and then zoom straight for our faces and food. They were carrying bacteria that if touched would make anyone sick. We named it the Bucca Bug, which sent many of our best soldiers running to the nearest outhouse. Miraculously, I did not get sick even once, being extremely cautious about what I touched and always keeping my hands sanitized and away from my mouth.

Through various media channels, I continued to hear reports of accusations of prisoners being ill-treated by American soldiers. Self-serving human rights activists took every opportunity to cry foul play as they looked for any excuse to condemn our methods of handling prisoners. We were accused of making them live in tents in extreme temperatures, forcing them to eat substandard food, and making them endure sandstorms, snakes, scorpions, and crowded quarters. Welcome to Iraq. Where did they think all the US military personnel were living? American soldiers were surviving under the same conditions, side-by-side with the prisoners, and no one was lamenting *our* misery.

Temperatures hit 145°F in Bucca

The military went to great lengths to care for these prisoners of war. Upon arrival they were deloused and cleaned up. The prisoners were given new sky-blue jumpsuits to wear, food they liked to eat, and any necessary medical treatment. Outside of a few harsh words or a push of an unruly prisoner by the guards, our team of interrogators treated the prisoners appropriately, as we were trained to do. We were committed to honoring the rules established in the Geneva Convention. I never witnessed torture being used as a means to get someone to talk. Except for a few, the prisoners we dealt with were very willing to cooperate with us, the majority having surrendered right at the beginning of the war.

* * *

I had been an interrogator for thirty-four years and had received extensive training in the advanced art of interrogation, learning how to use the most effective psychological approaches to break an individual and obtain vital information quickly. The tactics used by military interrogators are very different from the brutal, strong-arm tactics often portrayed by Hollywood and assumed by the media. I am sure there are interrogators that worked outside of the military guidelines. But all of the interrogators I worked with operated professionally, with a clear understanding of what constituted appropriate conduct and in absolute adherence to that standard.

My assignment at Camp Bucca was to work with a select group of high-ranking Iraqi officers, especially the generals. Each night after finishing my regular duties, a small group of us went out to the Hoover 7 Prisoner Compound to sit and talk with a most auspicious group of POWs, a group which included fifteen Iraqi generals and perhaps twenty-five or more colonels. Most of them had done what was suggested in leaflets that were airdropped prior to the war. They surrendered during the opening days of the war and had been POWs ever since. In most cases, they laid down their weapons without firing a shot, turned over their equipment and bases, instructed their men to return to their homes, and drove out to meet our oncoming forces.

There were over eleven thousand brigadier generals or above in the Iraqi Army (compared to three hundred in the US Army). Of these, only fifteen actually turned themselves in to us. The really bad guys didn't surrender but instead ran back to their houses, where they went into hiding. The good guys surrendered and expected they would be treated well, expedited through the process, and returned to their homes soon.

The routine was simple. We waited until 8:00 PM, when it was getting dark and cooling down a bit. A small tarp was placed on the ground in the middle of the compound, where I sat with three or four other interrogators, surrounded by thirty or forty Iraqi prisoners sitting cross-legged in the sand.

All fifteen of the generals were assigned to me and my group of interrogators. They were mine to coerce or persuade, to entice or compel, and to love or hate. I began to repeatedly interrogate each one of them until every bit of information had been gleaned from them. They were now my boys. My interpreter and I would be there with them on a daily basis until I knew everything there was to know about them.

We determined, at least with this group, whose situation and condition of capture was quite different, that the best way to extract accurate intelligence was to build a certain degree of trust and confidence with them. As the relationship developed, they began to share valuable bits and pieces of information. Consequently, the interrogation strategy evolved into more of a friendly approach with these men as we built rapport, mutual respect, and trust.

Frankly, I was impressed with the caliber of these men. For the most part they seemed to be good men with good intentions, who were anxious to get back to their families and to assist in the process of rebuilding their country. Several of the officers spoke English quite well, and most of the rest spoke enough English to get by in a limited fashion. I became close to a few of them as I spoke with them during my evening meetings, night after night.

As the prisoners gathered around us in a circle, we discussed a wide range of topics in great detail: their fate, what was expected of them, how they could help us, and what it would take before they could be released. We asked them questions, followed up on new leads, and confirmed their stories.

These important prisoners were surprisingly humble about their circumstances. Their greatest concern was to find out anything about the status of their families. We sincerely wanted to make their lives a little more bearable and were earnest in our desire to help them get released and home to their loved ones.

We worked with the Red Cross to get in touch with their families to alleviate any worry these officers might have. Some of them, who surrendered early in the war, were worried that Saddam, learning of their surrender, had killed their wives and children. I am also sure that many of the families imagined their beloved husbands and fathers had been killed in the fighting by the Americans. Some had as many as nine children; others had serious medical problems needing treatment. All were concerned for the welfare of their families.

I had been out driving beyond the boundaries of our base a few times and had been able to see the Iraqis living in the area. Overall, the response from the locals was very positive. No matter where I went, there were crowds of kids out on the streets waiting for an American to drive by, hoping to catch our attention or—even better—a bottle of water or something to eat.

The kids often stood on the side of the road, patiently waiting and enduring the heat of the day. When they saw us coming, they would begin to wave enthusiastically and then hold up the peace sign or give us a thumbs up as we passed, always with big smiles on their faces. Sometimes they yelled out English phrases, obviously picked up from other passing troops, phrases like "I love you" or "Give me water." The crowds of children were often peppered with adults, perhaps a parent or two, who had also come out to wave to the US military personnel. Adding to the boisterous welcome, cars full of Iraqis would often drive by, honking their horns and waving their arms.

People greeting us with a smile and a thumbs-up.

Despite their cheery greetings, it was difficult for me to see the children playing in their harsh environment. They flew along the dirty streets in tattered clothes, using sticks and stones as their only toys. I never saw a soccer ball, toy truck, doll, or any other toy. Yet such a life was all these children had ever known, and with a smile on their faces they made the most of their bleak situation. My heat ached for them.

The military had to be careful, especially with the kids that hung out on the sides of the roads. They would stand in the middle of the road, even lying down at times, in an effort to get us to stop. They usually sent out the smallest, cutest kid so that they could encircle the vehicle and try to steal things from inside. The bigger kids usually went right for open windows or any doors that weren't locked and then just started grabbing stuff. Their actions seemed prompted more by curiosity and childlike playfulness than out of any malicious intent; still, their actions posed a risk to them and to us. Despite the warm welcome, in the back of my mind there was a lingering concern that those who might want to hurt us could appear at any time, even in what appeared to be a welcoming throng.

* * *

As a rule of thumb, whenever we went out to Hoover 7, we would take cold drinks and treats for our prisoners. Of course, I wondered if it meant more to us than it did to them, given the fact they had lived their entire lives without cold drinks anyway. But they always enjoyed it when we brought along a snack like flatbread and hummus.

The old adage of "You catch more bees with honey than vinegar" rang true in Iraq too. It didn't take us long to realize that we could gain trust and cooperation, even of prisoners of war, through treating them with respect and kindness. With the exception of three individuals, the generals were all remarkably cooperative, providing us with valuable intelligence that resulted in greater success in many areas of the battlefield.

Once the generals were vetted, ("vetting" involves investigating someone thoroughly, especially in order to ensure that they are suitable for a job requiring secrecy, loyalty, or trustworthiness), we did everything in our power to address their needs, trying to make their stay in Hoover 7 as painless as possible. Given our extremely limited resources and the fact that we were also living in tents in the middle of the Iraqi desert, there wasn't a whole lot we could do other than providing them access to some local Iraqi food, medical care, the opportunity to write letters to their loved ones, and on occasion a way to actually speak directly with their family members over a phone.

With the amount of time I was spending out in Hoover 7, it

didn't take long before I began to understand, to a certain degree, the Iraqi psyche. Fairly quickly, I was able to identify like-minded and like-hearted individuals amongst the group, people to whom I took an immediate liking. Even so, we treated each man with full dignity and respect, acknowledging them as the generals they were. Perhaps it was our sincerity and our genuine concern for their well-being that won their hearts and minds, but whatever the reason, kindness begat kindness, and they reciprocated our actions in many small ways. I can honestly say, with no reservation, we grew to love them as our brothers.

* * *

On two consecutive evenings that May, I interviewed General Saif, a high-ranking general in the Iraqi Air Force. I spent about three hours each night going over information and questioning him in great detail. He was beyond cooperative. His demeanor was kind and gentle; his conduct was respectful and polite. He was never annoyed by the constant probing, being ever so patient and considerate. It was time well spent and generally very productive. It wasn't that the information I was able to extract was earth-shattering, but a bond was created and a relationship developed.

I took another interrogator, a twenty-seven-year-old soldier as my note-taker, and a middle-aged Iraqi woman from the US as my interpreter. The four of us sat on makeshift chairs or in the sand inside a small military tent that was usually occupied by the military police (MPs). I walked General Saif through his story from the beginning, attempting to extract each and every detail. I pursued every lead, every inkling of intelligence, until I exhausted each diversion or branch of information, which then usually led me down a variety of other courses and directions. It was a painstakingly exhaustive process, but methodical and systematic.

When the military questioning was over, we began talking about our families. General Saif became quite emotional as he started to speak of his wife and children, not knowing if they were still alive. He said he didn't mind staying at the POW camp as long as he was needed, but he just wanted some kind of assurance that his family was alive and well. He invited us to visit when the war was over and he was back home with his family, perhaps before we left to go back to the States. General Saif was sincere about helping us in any way he could. He was intent on giving us anything he could that might be of value to us.

As we walked him back into the compound where all the other officers were kept, we had an opportunity to sit for a moment with the other generals intermixed with a colonel or two. Each of us sat on a water jug as a chair, with the other generals standing around us. We spoke of God, the purpose of life, and the importance of having faith in God. They wondered out loud if God was punishing them for something they had done in the past. I suddenly saw them in a different light as we shared these deep personal feelings about our relationship with God. I told them that I was a better person for having met them and that my life would never be the same after having so many meaningful experiences with them. They agreed by nodding their heads and in unison expressed their appreciation for what my team had done for them. I found tears in my eyes as I heard their words. I said to myself, "These are my brothers."

As we said our good-byes and walked back to our Humvee, my young note-taker expressed his emotions in just a few simple words. He said he had been trying to figure out why he had come to Iraq, and tonight he had found the answer. He was anxious to get home to proclaim his newfound appreciation for people, for freedom, and for the blessings he had taken for granted.

Even our interpreter commented on the special spirit that was felt and how touched she was by the whole experience. She commented on how proud her father would have been. When he was alive, he had been arrested and tortured by Saddam on three different occasions. We all walked away feeling we had just had one of those rare life experiences. There was a spiritual kinship in our midst that was felt by everyone.

CHAPTER SIX

THE GOOD LUCK GENIE CAMPAIGN

O ne day, about the middle of May, 2003, as I was driving around with Major Price, we decided to see if we couldn't do something good for someone. As we were contemplating the possibilities, we noticed a soldier walking along the side of the road who looked like he could use a lift. We paused and asked him if he needed a ride; he smiled and jumped right in.

As we were making small talk with him, I told him, "Today is your lucky day, because you had the good fortune of getting in the Good Luck Genie's Hummer." We had just been to the PX (the Post Exchange), and I had an ice-cold pudding for him. I had just received a package from my work with the latest Sports Illustrated Swimsuit Edition, which I was willing to part with, reluctantly. Major Price and I decided that one of the best ways to bring happiness to ourselves was to do kind things for others. We surely made a difference in that soldier's day. This action was the start of the "Good Luck Genie Campaign."

Major Price, who had become my cohort in this venture, decided to visit one of the Iraqi families that the base had taken in for assistance and refuge. The family we picked had five children, all under the age of nine. One of their daughters had a brain tumor and seemed to be mentally handicapped. We took over some cold water, cookies, candy, and a box of crackers. They were so excited to see us drop in with all the goodies. We sat for a moment and spoke to

them, not with words, but with caring. They could sense our love for
their little children. This family had been decimated by Saddam's
brutal regime. They only knew a few words in English, and I knew
just a few words in Arabic. But it didn't matter; we connected with
them. As our eyes met, we shared a joyful moment that transcended
language.

In a small way, we were playing a part in a much larger plan. The
little things we did made a difference, although it wasn't apparent at
first. Great things do come about by small means. It was difficult to
say what effect our acts of kindness might have in the long run. Who
knew what lasting impression might be made on the future leaders
of this country?

Every day when things slowed down in the afternoon, Major
Price and I put on our wings and transformed into the Good Luck
Genies. We rode around deliberately doing good things for other
people we saw. Whether we were delivering treats, giving rides, or
telling jokes, we were successful in spreading some cheer.

We drove to the small nearby town of Umm Qasr to check on
the situation of the local populace. There were many kids out on the
streets hoping to see an American drive by so they could wave, say
hello, and stand close enough to the road to slap our outstretched
hands as we drove by (which sometimes really hurt!). They had been
neglected for decades by a country pumping its wealth toward fuel-
ing an oppressive government and a bloated military and lining the
pockets of its corrupt leaders. Little had been spent on even the most
basic needs of these people.

For the most part, the people lived in mud huts—adobe brick
homes with no amenities. There appeared to be no infrastructure, no
public systems, no industry of any kind, and very few shops or stores.
The town of Umm Qasr didn't even have its own water supply. The
water had to be trucked in from other areas to be distributed at water
points by large tankers. As we drove around the streets, mothers and
children lined the sides, asking for even the remaining portion of the
water bottles we carried around in our vehicles.

There was so much we wanted to do for these people, just to
help them get their city up and running. We would have started by
helping them to develop a water source for their town. As a group

of citizen soldiers, we had many skills that we could have shared with them from our experiences in life back home: construction, engineering, business, manufacturing, and farming. The possibilities were limitless.

There was so much we wanted to do to win the hearts and minds of these people by caring enough to share, to teach, and to make their lives better. We needed nothing more than sincere kindness. It was the only way we were going to connect with these people, penetrating through years of misinformation, brainwashing, and bad publicity regarding the US military. More than anything our intentions were from the heart, with real intent and concern for the well-being of the people. We all believed in the basic goodness of mankind.

And more than anything, I felt bad for the children, who seemed to have been totally forgotten along way. Under the glaring rays of the midday sun in the heat of the summer, children could be seen running about in the barren sands surrounding Umm Qasr, kicking rocks and throwing sticks, without even a bottle of water to quench their thirst. As we drove about the city side streets, I often contemplated their plight, an activity that further stirred up a desire to help them somehow, if even in the smallest of ways. I realized that, more that anything else, it was the hearts and minds of the Iraqi children, those of the rising generation, that were at stake in this conflict. At some point the cycle needed to be broken. I wasn't sure how I was going to accomplish this newfound mission, but I was sure there was a way to win them over, and I was determined to find it.

* * *

At the end of May 2003, President Bush declared an end to major combat operations. But the war was far from over. The fighting had shifted to a guerrilla-type campaign by an organized Iraqi insurgency. Suicide bombings, sniper attacks, and ambush attacks on checkpoints and convoys became an increasing threat. It had also been a month of sweltering heat and of uninterrupted sweating. Every pore in my body was a continuously leaking faucet. From the minute I woke up in the morning until I lay down at night, my clothes were soaked with sweat. We ended up drinking about six or seven full two-liter bottles of water every day—about three gallons. Fortunately, the mess hall was equipped with air conditioning, so at least while we were eating we could cool down.

The uncomfortable nighttime heat was a constant battle for me; without sufficient rest, I would be useless the next day. I had a small fan blowing the sultry air around the room, which at least evaporated some of the sweat that stained my shirt. It was a standard-issue brown T-shirt that looked like it had been tie-dyed; the design was created by the swirls of salt stains from a day of non-stop sweating. The wind, which howled like a furnace in a foundry and felt hot enough to melt steel, finally died down, making it possible to drift off to sleep.

Often, at dusk, I would sit slumped in a chair in my room, if you could call it a room. It was actually more like a cellblock. It was a section of the bombed-out radio station that could be seen from anywhere in camp. A scented candle flickered on my table. I could smell the sweet fragrance of cookies and spice, which was almost able to overcome the stomach-churning smells of the camp.

Each night I climbed the ladder, pillow and poncho in hand, to reach my resting spot. The addition of floodlights lit up the whole area, including the roof of my building, making it more difficult to sleep at night. The small mattress I slept on resembled a baby crib mattress, only a little longer. There was a constant layering of sand that piled up on my mattress and around the roof throughout the day. I could only imagine how much sand I inhaled daily. I was surprised I didn't cough up mud-balls from the depths of my lungs.

With the heat came the flies. Fly strips hung around most rooms in an attempt to put a dent in the fly population. These flies were unusually aggressive, swarming around my head and face whenever I was trying to get something done. Lizards would often dash across the floor, hoping to get lucky by snatching one of the low-flying pests. The lizards may have owned our room, but we were waging a successful war on the snakes and scorpions, which filled the camp. We made a small dent in the mouse population, killing three in one day with the traps we set out. Peanut butter was the bait of choice.

Even the troublesome desert pests provided opportunities for the generals and I to become better acquainted. Over the weeks of summer, the prisoners became increasingly worried about the number of scorpions and snakes infiltrating their area. Every time we went out to Hoover 7, they let us know how many they had seen or killed, all in an effort to convince us to provide them cots to sleep on, up off the ground. We empathized and were soon able to comply with their continual requests. Seeing the jubilation in their faces when the cots arrived was like watching a child opening Christmas presents. They were overjoyed, openly expressing their appreciation for our ability to actually address their true needs and concerns.

I continued to try and provide as many comforts for these men as I could. As we received our daily ice delivery, I made sure we had an extra bag to take out to the prisoners so they could at least enjoy a cold drink once in a while. I was working with Major Garrity, who seemed to be on the same wavelength, intent on doing the right thing by these men. Several times we met out there at the same time with ice bags in hand, both of us making an effort to ease the discomfort of those good men.

* * *

My happiest day since arriving at Camp Bucca came on a Sunday. I was working in the office writing up some interrogation reports. My rooftop bunk buddy came running in, beckoning me to follow him quickly over to the building next door. I jumped up quickly, stopped everything I was doing, and fast-stepped it next door, not sure what all the fuss was about.

I entered the briefing room just in time to see one of the generals from Hoover 7 sitting in the room with a woman and a young man, whom I immediately realized were his wife and son. I threw my arms around them all, greeting his family with the universal language of an embrace. He and I had been close for some time, so I was glad he wanted to share that moment with me. It was marvelous to see him be reunited with his family, even briefly.

There had been no official contact with the wife and son; they just showed up at the front gate, thinking that perhaps their husband and father might be held captive inside this POW camp. He had really been down, not knowing what might have happened to them. Now everything had changed. Even though he was not going to be able to leave, at least he knew his family was safe. He had been quite a whiner, in a depressed state for some time; but he became a new man from that moment on, with a twinkle back in his eye and a ready smile on his face.

I had the opportunity to speak about my experience in church services later that same day. I think I learned, at that very moment, what kind of joy the Savior might have been talking about when he said, "Man is that he might have joy." It is really hard to put into words that kind of happiness, unless you have experienced it firsthand. The joy that comes from losing yourself in service to others—and sharing in another person's true and honest happiness—is indescribable. As I thought back about the events of the day, I noticed that my reaction was so spontaneous and so natural; I didn't even have to think about it. The minute I saw him with them, I knew exactly what was going on, and at that instant I was filled with an overflowing of joy for him. I ran into the room, threw my arms around them, and greeted his family with the biggest smile on my face.

* * *

Events like that encouraged us to keep up our work as the Good Luck Genies. One day, we started out by procuring a box of apples—okay, we stole them—along with a few bags of ice and some flatbread, which we took out to our officer prisoners in Hoover 7. It was worth doing just to see the looks on their faces.

As fun as these moments were, the Good Luck Genies were there to help anyone in need, not just the prisoners of Hoover 7. On many occasions, the US military guards themselves received cold drinks and chips from the Genies. With everything they were required to endure—the smell, the prisoners, the heat, the sand, and so on—we had no doubts that they really deserved a well-earned treat now and then.

On another occasion, I took Steve, a willing accomplice and member of my team, out to Hoover 7 loaded with a shovel and some Styrofoam. We proceeded to build a homemade cooler for the high-ranking officers, so their ice wouldn't melt the minute we dropped it off. We loaded their new cooler with some ice, placed some water jugs in it, put the lid on, covered it with a tarp, and told them to enjoy. I also dropped off some potatoes and onions for them to cook up as an addition to their daily dose of boring food.

Our kindness was consistently returned. One of the generals whom I had grown quite close to, an infantry commander named Matta, told me through his friend that he had a gift for me. Of course, I told him that I didn't need a gift of any sort; all I wanted was the news that they would be released. He was determined to present me with his gift. He gave me his prayer beads, with 103 beads. This took me by surprise, since I knew how much those meant to him. Prayer beads were a part of the people, like a baby would hold onto a pacifier; they were forever counting and rubbing their beads. I was deeply touched by his gesture of kindness.

I wasn't expecting my birthday to be different from any other day in Camp Bucca. But while I was sitting at the computer at 6:30 a.m., a few of the men came in singing "Happy Birthday" and holding a plate full of cake pieces they had lifted from the mess hall the night before. There was a lonely toothpick burning on top of one of the pieces. Steve, who was my son's age, had written me a brief note, thanking me for my example and leadership. I was touched by his thoughtfulness and his kind words complimenting me for all I had done.

That evening, we returned to Hoover 7 for our discussions. A few of the prisoners, once they saw me, returned quickly to their respective tents, only to return moments later with a small envelope. One of them had taken the time to actually make a ribbon out of paper from a brown sack that he taped to the top of the envelope. Someone had told them that it was my birthday. They had written a short letter wishing me the best of birthdays and long life for many more. They apologized for not being able to give me anything more, but I assured them that their friendship and thoughtful letters were more than I could have hoped for.

One of the generals gave me a small box of breath mints, which he wrapped in white lined paper. I was startled by such an expression. Mustering composure, I thanked him from the bottom of my heart for his kind gesture, putting my hand on my heart hoping that he would understand. I later read the letters when I returned to the privacy of my room, knowing I might be overcome with emotion.

I was on a journey to rediscover myself in Iraq. It was an evolution of the self through deliberate actions and abundant service. My biggest leaps forward in the process seemed to occur when I lost myself in the concerns of others.

Our seemingly insignificant acts of kindness to the prisoners and the US soldiers were often reciprocated at unexpected times. On one occasion, I was surprised by the arrival of two packages, sent from Michigan by two FedEx coworkers. It was such a treat, due not only to the personal goodies that were included but also the thoughtful items sent to share with the Iraqi children. I think that they must have been reading my mind and heart, and I am deeply grateful to all who have worked to ensure that every small kindness comes back around, full circle.

* * *

As the post-war season dragged on, I continued to be responsible for the high-ranking officers of Hoover 7. I was their advocate and their voice connecting them to the upper echelons of our command, which held the keys to their release. I was also the one who made a daily effort to extract any remaining bit of valuable information out of them. I had a mission that straddled both sides of the fence. I had a military obligation on one hand, a humanitarian mission on the other, and a determination to succeed at both.

Part of our humanitarian mission was to assist in reuniting or connecting the generals with their family members, reassuring them of each other's well being. On many occasions I had the luck and

Sign outside our camp in Hoover 7

good fortune of being able to do just that. One day two families, having visited several other POW camps, found their way to our camp, in hopes of finding their imprisoned family members. To our mutual surprise, their loved ones were there, at Camp Bucca. Once we made the connection, I was so excited I couldn't contain myself. I threw my arms around the prisoners, overcome with joy and happiness. They too were both overcome with emotion, sobbing uncontrollably. I tried to reassure the families that we would take good care of their men and try to get them released as soon as possible. The generals both had beautiful families with many beautiful children, some of whom even spoke English to some degree.

This same week turned out to be an especially wonderful one for me, in that two of my prisoners were finally released to go home. This small victory was such a long time coming that I couldn't hold back my excitement. A few other people that had been involved with the officers and I went out to the camp to tell them the good news. It was quite a moment, seeing their faces and the happiness in their eyes, or eye (one of them only had one eye), as the case may be. They rushed about, throwing together their meager belongings, beyond ready to go.

With the departure of these two men, I was able to take part in an Iraqi tradition, which I call the "rock-throwing ritual." Every one picks up seven rocks, which they throw behind the person who is leaving, meant to convey the message that the person is to leave for good, to never come back. In my zeal, I really got into the spirit of the moment, picking up the biggest rocks I could find and chucking seven of them at each person, telling them to leave and never come back. We took them down for out-processing, then to wait for their ride. We were able to say our good-byes and take a couple of pictures together. It was a great moment, and one I hoped to see repeated until we'd sent every one of those officers home.

These are the kind of moments that will stick in my heart for the rest of my life. I felt that this was what it was all about. Meeting their families and their children made the war and our efforts very personal, as I was able to see and experience firsthand the love that exists in a child's eyes. I knew the future of Iraq was in their hands.

* * *

One day, the Red Cross came through with messages from a few of the officers' families. What a miracle! And what a load off of my shoulders to hear the good news. The prisoners were relieved to know that the families that had been reached were all safe.

After seeing an ad in the newspaper for cell phones, with a phone number for the city of Mosul, the prisoners came up with an idea. They would call that number and have whoever answered the phone either call or go directly to the prisoner's home so that family members could get on the phone. I was delighted to discover that their plan actually worked. Using this strategy they were able to hook up an Iraqi Navy general with his family. Although some prisoners were able to receive comforting news from home, they were still frustrated by their continued detention.

CHAPTER SEVEN

FRIENDS IN NEED

As soon as I answered the phone, I knew it was trouble. The guards at the front checkpoint informed me that there was a bunch of upset family members wanting to visit their loved ones. Normally, we allowed family visits on Thursdays, Fridays, and Saturdays. But this week, due to an increase in the threat level and the lack of MP support, all visitations were canceled. But nobody bothered to tell the families.

Many of these family members had driven halfway across the country to visit their loved ones, only to find out that all visitations were canceled for the week. Many of them had spent their last bit of money just to pay for the round-trip taxi ride.

Someone had to diffuse the situation. I went out with an interpreter to try to explain the situation to some very disappointed people. I felt bad but was forced to comply with the camp commander's decision. I offered to take the bags of food they had brought for their family members and any messages they might have. It was an unfortunate situation, one that really pulled on my heartstrings. I was usually a very accommodating person, willing to do whatever was needed to resolve a situation, but in this case my hands were tied.

Those were tough times for all, not just for the prisoners. All of us were away from our homes and families and had to face our own sacrifice and suffering. There were young men who had married right before they were mobilized, others who had a wife and small children, and some who left a pregnant wife and missed the birth of their first child. Additionally, there were many with financial crises or who had been called upon to interrupt their education. All of us were missing life back home.

Once regular visits were reinstated, a crowd started forming at the front gate early in the morning, much earlier than was required. I was not sure why they felt they had to get there so early. It was not like one family was going to get ahead of another or get to see their loved one longer than another. The crowd was generally unruly, one family trying to get in front of another, jockeying for position to see who was going to get on the bus first. The funny thing was that they all got on the bus at the same time.

I always went out to meet the families of the generals to ensure they got on the bus without any glitches and to pick up any bags of food or supplies they might have brought. With the generals' POW numbers in hand, I went through the crowd trying to identify those families with appointments to see one of the generals, hoping that I might make first contact with them. I tried to put their minds at ease, assuring them their loved ones were doing well.

By the time I was finished with the generals' families, my Hummer looked like a Meals on Wheels van—full of assorted bags, food, small suitcases, watermelons, and dates. Everybody brought dates. One of the families brought me a huge bag of dates to personally consume. I love dates—but not ten pounds of them. I gathered up bed sheets, pajamas, cakes, and huge containers of rice, all for the prisoners.

When I went out to the front gate, I saw the wife of one of the generals, whom I had met before. She wasn't on my list of those who had appointments, but even so I felt inclined to assist her in visiting her husband. After making a deal with the MPs, I arranged for her to get on the bus that would take her inside the camp, while I dashed over to Hoover 7 to pick up her husband.

The bus arrived at the visiting location prior to my departure for Hoover 7. When she saw me, she immediately demanded to know where her husband was, unappreciative of the big favor I was doing and unaware that I was working way outside of the box for her.

When I went to pick up her husband, he had a huge suitcase full of items he had received from the MPs: cookies, cheese, toiletries, paper items, and so on. I was concerned that he was abusing the system, asking for items from the guards and then saving them all for his family. I knew his intentions and concerns for his family were good and that his family could probably use the items, but whatever he took for his family ended up being taken away from some other prisoner, who perhaps went without.

As I drove the husband, General Saad, from Hoover 7 toward his wife in the waiting tent, I stopped the vehicle on the dirt road to have a couple of words with him. I told him, with kindness, that I hoped he understood what I was doing was outside of my normal duties and way outside of our camp rules. I didn't want him to expect this every week, and I wanted to make sure he appreciated this gesture of kindness. I observed the rules and regulations of the MP unit managing the camp. Most of what I did for the generals was a long way from being within my normal duties but was definitely not against the rules.

That night as I visited my generals, General Saad took me aside to offer up his prayer beads and several large rings as a token of appreciation for the many things I had done for him. He said he felt bad about the money I had given his wife the week before so she could return home from visiting him and for the many other acts of kindness performed. I wanted no gifts for my deeds, just a change of heart from him, to start thinking of others first, leaving his self-serving ways behind.

Imprisonment brings out the very worst and the very best in people. There were those who never asked for anything, always putting others before self. They were the same ones who never complained, never whined, and never cried about being there so long. They were the ones who made productive use of their time, finding ways to be productive in any situation. Those quiet but influential doers had an enormous impact on the lives of all those at Camp Bucca.

* * *

One evening, the generals were swarming around Major Price as he passed out a few special items he had been able to acquire. I took this opportunity to walk around the camp with General Saif. We walked side by side, back and forth, across the front of the pen, far out of hearing distance of other prisoners. I was always so moved by his comments and his generosity. While the others were grabbing up stuff from Major Price, General Saif declined to get anything for himself, saying that he would be last if there was anything left. Saif and the small group of men in his tent never asked for anything and were so humble about receiving things from us.

As we began our discussion, I felt a spiritual bond with him and commented on the way I was feeling. He concurred, stating he was feeling something different too. We shared a unique bond of friendship, full of mutual trust, respect, and admiration. He had been blessed with a great attitude—optimism, compassion, and humility—uncommon in most men, especially army generals.

He was elated by the news that Coalition forces were building on many of the ideas he had developed and presented to me. He was ecstatic, not because they had followed his advice, but because he truly felt they were headed down the right course. He was full of hope for the success of the Coalition's endeavors.

General Saif's next comments stunned me. He said he felt as if he was the student and I was the teacher. He felt he could learn so much from me and that together we could accomplish great things for the people of Iraq. I paused for a moment while casting my eyes down to my feet and feeling quite undeserving of his confidence in me. He reminded me of his pledge to be my shield from any would-be assailants if I were to go into Baghdad.

As I considered the task ahead, I felt truly inadequate in teaching him anything. I was the student who was learning from him. General Saif was a pillar of stone, unmoved by the forces of men who tried to shake his conviction. My emotions crept close to the surface as I recognized that a caring God was guiding our efforts and our lives.

* * *

After the war ended, there were thousands of criminals who had been released from prison by Saddam. Within ninety days of the start of the war, most military personnel held in Camp Bucca had been released. This left only two groups in the camp —the generals and colonels in Hoover 7 and the worst type of criminals, who had been murdering, stealing, raping, and committing various other crimes against the people of Iraq. What were we supposed to do with these criminals? Put them back on the streets of Iraq?

Regardless of their status, rank, or crimes, we fed the prisoners plenty of food twice a day, food prepared right next to where my food was prepared. We made every effort to provide them with food that was to their own liking, ethnic food as close to their own as possible, prepared by people from that region, purchased right from the local economy.

We gave them new T-shirts, new jump suits, additional clothing whenever needed, slippers, flip-flops, socks, and much more. They received plenty of supplies. They had soap, shampoo, towels, and many other personal necessities. They were provided with cots to sleep on, blankets when necessary, and cot mattresses if wanted. The medics came by every morning to see if they had any ailments to report. They had daily showers, plenty of water, soccer balls, and many other items for their comfort, enjoyment, and benefit.

Camp Bucca was a prisoner-of-war camp, now transitioning to being a prison. If you were to look at a list of why the men were being detained, you would see that most of them were there because they had either committed some violent crime or had attempted to attack or kill an American. Regardless of their crimes, we continued to believe in their human rights and made every effort to consider their needs.

I have seen interrogation teams from all over the world conducting interrogations, witnessed firsthand their approaches and techniques, which has only reconfirmed my belief that the United States of America is one of only a few countries that honors the Geneva Convention. Without a doubt, we treat our prisoners better than anyone else in the world. Even the Iraqi generals commented in surprise and admiration on the treatment they received from us. They certainly wouldn't have been treated like this by Saddam Hussein.

In our interrogations, I never witnessed any physical abuse of the prisoners. We never used torture as means to acquire information, unless you consider taking away a prisoner's cigarettes cruel and unusual. I did make a prisoner sit out in the sun once for an hour. All of our techniques involve psychological methods of extracting information, viewing torture as an inefficient method to break people. No doubt, information can be extracted through torture, but its truthfulness would be questionable. Gaining the prisoners' trust and respect is by far the most effective method for gathering intelligence.

Interrogation team at Hoover 7

Our objective was to get life-saving information out of these people in an expeditious manner. This did require us to use a variety of well-established approaches and strategies. We made every effort to silence and segregate the prisoners when necessary to ensure there was no collusion between prisoners. This might require us to hood them on occasion. We did strip search the prisoners to ensure they were not carrying any weapons. We had to keep them on edge, unsure of their fate and fearful of their treatment.

There were exceptions and isolated incidents, but those were few and far between. If there was any mistreatment, it was rare and not representative of the thousands of prisoners who had received the best possible treatment.

We lived in a strange place, far away from what we knew and were familiar with. We were under a lot of stress from the conditions and demands placed upon us in that environment. We were dealing with a very strange element. We were surrounded by far-from-normal fundamentalists, fanatics, extremists, and hardened criminals. We were away from our loved ones back home, working long hours with no days off. And more than anything, we were concerned about saving American lives.

I have seen nothing but the utmost respect for the prisoners' needs. In most cases, we went out of our way to ensure they were being handled appropriately. In many instances, I personally witnessed genuine acts of kindness displayed toward the prisoners.

* * *

In late July, word came down that I had to be in Baghdad by August 3. I tried to push back my departure date for another week or so in order to finish up a few important things, such as writing a few more letters to key individuals petitioning the generals' release, but there was no wiggle room.

Several of the generals had expressed a strong desire for me to stay with them until they were all released. They had pleaded with me to not allow anyone to move me until things had been resolved with their continued detention. I had tried to reassure them that no matter what, I would not forget them. I had grown close to so many of them. I had spent almost every night for three months getting to know them, seeing them at their worst and at their best, meeting their families, knowing their special needs, and working through bureaucratic frustrations. We were now brothers, held together with a bond uncommon in the course of most human lives.

I promised to continue the fight for their release, which was even more likely given the nature of my new assignment. I was moving to Baghdad to work at the top of the food chain, with all the bigwigs who were running the country. What better place for me to work for the generals' release. To me, it seemed an answer to my prayers.

CHAPTER EIGHT

LIFE IN THE PALACE

If I had tried to concoct the most dramatic change of assignment possible in Iraq, Bucca to Baghdad would have been it. Camp Bucca was about as far from the center of Iraq as possible, in the south near the Kuwaiti border and Iraq's sliver of a coastline. The area near Camp Bucca had been shunned by Saddam and his oil largess. The radio tower next to my sand-infested office and rooftop dormitory was about the most opulent architectural masterpiece Saddam ever bestowed on that desolate part of Iraq.

But now I was in Baghdad, smack-dab in the middle of the administrative epicenter of the new Iraq. Of Saddam's many presidential palaces, I was stationed in the main governmental palace in what was once the nucleus of his regime. After the fall of Saddam, this place was called the Coalition Provisional Authority (CPA) Headquarters and was center stage for the Coalition's military and governmental operations. It was a massive complex of colossal, oversized buildings, all erected according to Saddam's presidential style. But all the marble, high ceilings, chandeliers, and handcrafted decorations in the world could never compensate for his lack of good taste. The difference between opulence and bad taste is that opulence has its limits. In Saddam's Iraq, bad taste hit new lows.

The CPA Headquarters was at the center of the Green Zone. Everything within a one-mile radius emanating from the CPA was considered a safe area. The area, consisting of governmental buildings and housing, was cleared of would-be attackers and was secured, monitored, and patrolled by US troops twenty-four hours a day.

My new position pushed me in a different direction. I was a strategic debriefer at the CPA. With the war's major combat operations completed, we were no longer capturing prisoners of war. Most of the POWs had been released, thus bringing about the change in my mission. As a debriefer, I interviewed people that had information they wanted to voluntarily share with the Coalition. These were average Iraqi citizens who had seen something, heard something, or knew something of importance relating to criminal activities, weapons, potential attacks, corruption, or any other activity against Coalition forces or the Iraqi people.

A good debriefer has a skill set similar to those of an interrogator, except the debriefer doesn't need to break the subject or force them to talk by using certain approaches. The debriefer instead needs to determine the credibility of the source and the shared information.

Many good Iraqis were stepping forward to bring us information about activities going on against Coalition forces. Every day, people came to our office to inform us of activities in their community that were illegal, were pro-Saddam, or were in opposition to Coalition forces. We gathered the information from the sources and, as directed by General Sanchez, pushed the information to action. The required action would typically involve dispatching a team of Special Forces to conduct a raid on the location reported by the sources. These raids were conducted nightly, often resulting in more information and more leads.

****

More gratifying than the opulence of my new surroundings was being able to work side by side with my long-time friend Chief Allen. America's first battle with Saddam brought us together in 1991 in Saudi Arabia during Desert Storm. We were similar in temperament, personality, and motivation. We had a synergy and compatibility that made working together an adventure in discovery and personal fulfillment.

Chief Allen and I were fortunate enough to snag a large, second-floor office for our two linguists and us. The office was about forty feet long and twenty feet wide and was lit by two crystal chandeliers hanging from fifteen-foot ceilings. There were three large windows from which we could see one of the four large sculptured heads of

Saddam that guarded the four corners of the building. But the centerpiece of our office was the Mother of All Desks. I'm sure it was originally slated for a much larger and more important office, perhaps for Ambassador Bremer. But for now it was all ours. Fortunately, we were able to procure six large high-backed chairs, perfect for dealing with the number of sources we had to talk to on a daily basis.

In spite of the palatial setting, I was actually humbled by the broad scope of the mission and the endless possibilities of this new assignment. It provided a degree of flexibility that allowed me to call upon my own ingenuity and creativity to come up with solutions. I could develop new ways of gathering human intelligence from a variety of sources. The whole city of Baghdad was my playground. I was ready for this new challenge and hoped I was up to the task.

* * *

Home was a small but comfortable trailer located on the palace compound. As I sat on a real bed listening to my boom box, I could reach over to my mini-fridge and grab a bottle of ice-cold water, all in a room cooled to a perfect temperature by my own AC unit. I almost felt guilty—almost.

The comforts of the palace shielded us from many of the natural elements of the desert, but when we went outside, there was still the oppressive heat to contend with. Any time we ventured beyond the walls of our compound, we were required to wear full battle rattle, which was never comfortable but always comforting.

On my first full day at the palace, I went out with one of our collection teams to familiarize myself with the neighborhoods of Baghdad and scope out the area. We drove all over this sprawling city of five million people. I was able to witness firsthand the nature and the extent of the damage inflicted by the weaponry of the US military. It was quite a tribute to the precision of our bombing to drive through a neighborhood and see only the targeted buildings completely demolished while adjacent buildings remained unscathed. Never during our day of driving around Baghdad did I see any evidence that our bombs had missed their targets, inadvertently hitting a house or a school or other civilian areas.

My interpreter continually remarked about how the city of

Baghdad had changed since he was there many years ago. "The city used to be beautiful and clean, modern for its time, some twenty to thirty years ago," he said. "The city is now showing its age from the years of neglect and the scars of war. It's dirtier and more run down."

There was very little color to the buildings; a sandy khaki color dominated the landscape. There was a lot of trash and garbage on the sidewalks and streets, showing that not all services were operating.

Most of the city appeared to be up and running with electrical power restored. Although some of the shops and businesses were not yet open, many were, indicating that people were attempting to recover from a season of disruption caused by war. I was pleasantly surprised to see the people bustling around, busily engaged in shopping, work, and other daily activities. The streets were full of cars and people, even congested at times, which was somewhat frightening in a land where traffic laws are widely disregarded.

We were always aware that at any moment an unseen assailant from a window or rooftop could light us up. We never forgot, even for a second, the ever-present danger of the areas we were traveling in—our loaded rifles were ready to fire. We were careful not to get blocked in by any of the traffic, using our Hummer's ability to drive over obstacles or to change direction immediately when the traffic started to jam up. After driving these streets daily for a few weeks, we started feeling comfortable about driving around in the middle of the day. I trusted the team chief's instinct regarding the degree of danger we were facing at any given moment.

At one safe area, we stopped to grab a few cold drinks from a friendly street vendor, who, along with other Iraqi citizens, thanked us for our willingness to come to their rescue. A man parked his car for a moment to buy some meat hanging in a butcher shop, so with my interpreter, I walked over to share some small talk with a young boy who had been left in the car. The boy, Talib, said he was six years old. In his cute smile and expressive eyes, I could see a bright future.

The owner of the butcher shop came out to speak with us and spoke English quite well. He was curious about our presence in his neighborhood, but more than anything wanted to show off his ability to speak English. He said he used to teach at the university. He

65

was quick to inform me that he was a Christian and no longer afraid to admit that.

Throughout our Baghdad excursion, we were greeted by the friendly waves and smiles of people on the street. Supposing they might be afraid of an imposing military vehicle and our weapons, I made a special effort to wave to everyone I could see as we drove around; I was making an effort to win over the Iraqi people any way I could.

A few days later, I had the opportunity to board a Black Hawk helicopter taking us to a meeting north of Baghdad. From my perch in the sky, I was able to get a full view of what Iraq was really all about. As I left the city, I saw an expanse of farms, fields, date palm groves, and countryside stretching toward the horizon. I saw herds of goats, cows, and sheep grazing in sparse fields of hay.

As we continued our flight farther north, the cultivated green landscape gave way to more barren grazing land. There were adobe houses grouped together in flat-roofed villages, all sharing the same khaki color. The farmhouses appeared poor, at times without power or running water. I saw canals bringing water from the two major rivers nearby, the Tigris and the Euphrates. Children would run out of their houses to wave as we passed overhead.

* * *

Every night the sound of gunshots echoed throughout the city, reminding me of the ever-present danger that lurked around every corner. This random unpredictability kept us on our toes, wondering with every explosion if perhaps one of our fellow soldiers had just fallen.

Some days were worse than others as far as the number of attacks. Sometimes it was soldiers just being out at the wrong time in the wrong areas or behaving carelessly. Other times it was a car bomb or a remote-controlled detonation on a bridge or street.

The insurgent weapon of choice had become the Improvised Explosive Device (IED). An IED is a homemade device that can be detonated to kill, maim, or harass anyone unfortunate enough to be nearby. An IED can be contained in almost anything—a milk carton, a can of soda, a dog carcass, a car, or a trash bag. An IED can be placed on the roadside, stashed in a pothole, taped to a car, stuffed in a building, set on a bridge, or strapped to a person. Occasionally, they are simply tossed from a moving vehicle. IEDs can be time-delay triggered, command detonated by wire, or remotely detonated by a cell-phone, pager, doorbell button, key-fob, or toy-car remote. An IED can use homemade, commercial, or military explosives alone or in combination with toxic chemicals, biological toxins, or radiological material. Every IED is viciously unique in its design, manufacture, application, and potential for mayhem.

In 2004 there were almost 12,000 known IED-related incidents. For a small-time insurgent, an IED was less expensive than an AK-47, easier to put into action, and able to deliver more bang for the buck. Sometimes they were used simply to harass and discredit the security forces in Baghdad. Frequently they were used to entice Coalition forces into prepared ambushes. They were often used to target individuals or groups, also claiming the lives of countless civilians who happened to be standing in the way.

While I was there, IEDs became the single greatest threat Coalition forces faced in Iraq. Increasingly, they were also used against Iraqis who were cooperating with the Coalition, causing distrust and instability and fear. This underscored the value of gathering intelligence regarding these insidious and destructive devices. Whenever one was located and disarmed, we knew lives had been saved.

Thankfully, there were many safe areas around the city and the attacks were isolated. Most neighborhoods were peaceful and virtually without incident.

We received leads on who these terrorists were, and in many cases we were able to take them down. On one of my first nights in Baghdad, we were able to catch up with a Fedayeen officer who had been terrorizing a neighborhood. It was a time-consuming process involving considerable assistance from the locals who were gaining confidence in our ability to provide security for Iraq. As the days went by, the locals trusted us more and more, which was evident by the number of people stepping forward to provide us with information.

We had numerous individuals stepping forward to divulge information, but many times their real intent was to request a job, a favor, or reimbursement for their time and expenses. I started to feel like everyone was looking to take care of themselves under the pretense of serving their country.

We had to assume ulterior motives unless our experience proved otherwise. I wasn't able to fully trust the information that was being shared by these sources until we had made some determination of their integrity and desire to serve their country. I recognized that many of these individuals were just trying to survive in a very difficult environment. Some of the Iraqi people were so desperate that for a handful of cash they were willing to fire on a soldier, blow up a tank, or set an explosive on a bridge. The various anti-Coalition groups were basically hiring poor peasants to pull the trigger to kill our soldiers. Many of those people served whatever side would pay them the most.

Day after day, we continued to meet with people who wanted to share information they had regarding things going on in the city. I was amazed by the number of absurdly bogus reports we received from people attempting to milk the system or get something for nothing. At times I wondered if I had the word "sucker" written in Arabic on my forehead. At times the information was just not as valuable as the person thought or didn't result in the compensation they were expecting.

Debriefing an informant

One gentleman who assisted us was disappointed with the job offer we gave him, believing he was owed something more to his liking. I was disappointed with his attitude after I felt we had done all we could do. He gave no indication that he appreciated anything we were offering him, not even in a polite way of acknowledging our efforts. At times, I wondered if I would be able to remain compassionate as I continued to deal with my fair share of liars, ingrates, weaklings, bums, and sycophants.

Other times, it seemed like I was in some kind of a parent-child relationship, trying to get the Iraqis to step up to the plate, to be responsible, to take advantage of opportunities, and to take some initiative. But we knew where these people had been and what kind of environment they had grown up in for the last two and a half decades. Each day we saw the human harvest of Saddam's repressive regime.

The minds of these people had been brainwashed for so long that there was a huge gap between them and us. One of our interpreters told us of a time, several years earlier, when he was walking along the side of the road and people threw things at him as they drove by because he held a guitar in his hand. They told him that he would go to hell for listening to Western music and playing a Western instrument. Americans have a long way to go before we begin to understand the mind-set of many Iraqis.

It was not that we wanted to force Western culture upon them, but rather that we wanted to assist them in creating an environment of freedom and responsibility where they could initiate positive changes without fear of reprisal. We wanted to help them improve their standard of living and open the doors to freedom, enabling them to take their rightful place in the free world.

Scattered among all of the self-serving people with their ulterior motives were many sincere, hard-working Iraqis who just wanted to get on with their lives and see their country prosper. I spoke with a restaurant owner who had come in to give us some information. I asked him about his business, given the current situation. He replied that business was really tough, especially without electricity, but any kind of business was better than life with Saddam. He invited us over to dine whenever we got a chance.

I also recall a mother and her daughter who had both found work in the new government. They were grateful for our efforts and invited us to spend some time at their farm on the outskirts of Baghdad, to enjoy some real home cooking and a boat ride on the Tigris River.

Two Iraqi policemen were kind enough to bring in some baked chicken, hummus, flatbread, olives, and pickled cucumbers. I relished every bite of it, appreciating their delicious offering, which was a pleasant change from our normal lunch of corn dogs or tuna fish sandwiches. They brought us enough to share with anyone else that had the good fortune of dropping in on our office picnic. We spread it out on the table normally used for maps and other more important matters.

Iraqis like these recognized that Americans brought hope to this land and its people. Freedom and hope are contagious, and I made it my aim to spread that light to every Iraqi I came in contact with. Americans are an optimistic people, and we are eager to share freedom with the world. As one British interrogator said to me, "You Americans really do have hope for this land, don't you?" You bet your life we do.

* * *

In coming to my new position at the CPA, I was blessed to be working for the US Army general responsible for approving the discharge of the Iraqi generals still held at Camp Bucca. I continued to actively push forward the meticulous paperwork necessary to secure their release. This required working through the many layers of military bureaucracy, completing each step with accuracy. After all the paperwork was submitted, twelve of my fifteen generals were approved for immediate release. This was wonderful for them, wonderful for their families, wonderful for me, and wonderful for the future of Iraq.

Still, working in Baghdad definitely had its drawbacks and dangers. On August 19 at around four in the afternoon, I was going about my work as usual when I heard and felt a large blast not too far away. Such were fairly common occurrences, and so I wasn't too alarmed by it at the time. Later, however, I returned to the office and found an unusual buzz around the operation center. I was shocked to learn that the explosion had occurred at the UN headquarters in a terrorist bombing. I was saddened to hear that numerous people had been killed and injured, including a number of innocent bystanders, people looking for work, and many others. I struggled to make sense of such random acts of violence, my worry for my fellow soldiers only increasing.

The most unsettling thing about the entire situation was the fact that many of the terrorists in Iraq were from outside of the country, people who had traveled there for the sole purpose of disrupting all efforts to give the Iraqi people a life free from fear, bondage, and torture. I found it disturbing to consider what kind of place would deliberately breed such contempt and hatred for others, hatred that knew no bounds or limitations and would stop at nothing to accomplish their goal of killing innocent human beings. Such blind hatred can seem powerful, overwhelming, and insurmountable, for the perpetrators as well as those watching around the periphery. My only consolation was that, visible or not, acknowledged or not, there was good being done every day.

Maybe our efforts for the most part were going unnoticed: the schools and hospitals that had been opened, the playgrounds and housing projects that had been started, and the many jobs that had been created. Where was all the talk about the thousands of good things that had been done? Why was the media not promoting the positive story of all great things happening day after day at the hands of the US military? Where was the truth in reporting that makes good news as salable as bad news?

My partner and I were tasked to go talk to the hundreds of people that were displaced by the bombing of the UN headquarters and the Rasheed Hotel. We were supposed to speak with any of them that wanted to talk to someone about what had happened or what they might have seen, hoping to provide the intelligence community with some leads. Told that many of them were slated to sleep over in our palace that night, we set up over 150 beds in the chapel in anticipation of their arrival. Not a single person showed up.

Then again, just a few days later we had so many people crowding into our office with information that we could barely hold them all. Under such frustrating circumstances, discouragement was always a constant threat. Being able to joke around and make fun of things helped us get through this extended time away from our families. Chief Allen and I had similar personalities and frequently played tag-team-humor with our Interpreters and sources, adding a little levity to our crazy days. For me, humor was a great anesthetic, numbing me from the stark reality of where we were and what we were doing. We just didn't want to take things too seriously, realizing that life for so many in Iraq was too painful to discuss. I think the truth of their bleak existence would be depressing to many in the States. I was astonished that they could go on for so long without any income; many of them had yet to return to any kind of paying work.

If someone was to ask me what was sustaining these people in such a harsh environment, I would have to say it was hope—hope of a new beginning with hope for a different future. One day while talking to one of our young Iraqi interpreters, he conveyed to me an incident he'd had with his family, who had asked about the Americans he was working with. He said, "The one thing that stood out about Americans was they seemed to have a lot of hope for things to come."

Then again, not everyone I met held on to hope in this way. In the course of my interviews with numerous sources, I was surprised by how many of them, young men and women in their thirties and forties, felt that their lives were on the downhill slide or basically over. It was astonishing to me how a young man in his early thirties could think for a moment that his life was going to always be the way it was, without much hope for anything different.

I had been asked numerous times how was I able to maintain a high level of hope during my stay in Iraq, how I was able to maintain a feeling of purpose and meaning in all that I had been doing. That question often caused me to think of how it is that some of us are able to maintain hope when all seems lost, while others lose hope for anything different. How it is that some are able to find purpose and meaning in whatever they are doing, while others hopelessly spend their time thinking of better days gone by? Where does hope come from? How do we obtain and sustain hope, and how do we give it to others?

I have come to the conclusion that hope is a divine gift that grows within us as our belief in a loving, caring Father in Heaven grows. I believe that hope grows from within us as we find purpose and meaning in all that we do, due to a belief that we are part of an eternal plan of progression. We hold the potential within ourselves for a powerful, driving force. If we will but tap into it, it will allow us to believe in our mission and our purpose for being. This force allows us to maintain optimism in every aspect of our lives, allows us to continue believing that there is purpose in all things, no matter where we are or what we are doing. I am not talking about blind hope or naive optimism. I am talking about a hope based on a belief system of planned events, a guided existence, which allows us to let hope grow within us to the point that it spills over into all that we do. This is not a passive hope; it is active, touching all aspects of our lives, because we believe in a Father who cares enough to be there with us.

This type of hope becomes a driving force compelling us to press forward, to drive through, and to engage life with a vengeance and a passion for living. More importantly, this active hope compels us to look diligently for purpose and meaning in our own life's activities.

This hope is contagious; it is infectious, even. People that are around it feel it and are affected by its radiating energy, compelling them to seek to make it their own. Others feel our hope expressed in word and deed, and they see it in our eyes. It swells within us and grows beyond us, spilling over into all that we touch. In the presence of this type of hope there is no room for disbelieving cynics, those who choose to criticize, find fault, dwell in negativity, or question the very reasons for why things turn out the way they do. For me, personally, I am sold on a hope-filled, meaningful journey, one taken together with a divine partner who loves me.

* * *

As usual, I was wakened early by the sound of the date palm branches outside scraping across the top of my trailer, dropping golden date nuggets on the roof. It sounded as if I were being pelted by shrapnel from a nearby explosion. As the bright rays of morning streamed through my trailer window, I felt there was hope for a new beginning for Iraq. I went to my knees to offer up the gratitude of my heart for all that was transpiring around me as I personally witnessed the remaking of a nation, humbly asking for help in being able to do my part in pushing this work forward. I knew we were not alone in our efforts. I rose from my knees, knowing that a strange parade of characters would soon be marching through my office.

One young man I had the privilege of working with was a former Free Iraq Fighter, looking to reestablish a life for himself in the new Iraq. Uncertainty about his future was making him feel quite lost; he was so depressed that it really touched my heart, inspiring me to try and help him as much as I could. To get him started, I took him over to the headquarters for his area in hopes that I might find a job for him. I spoke with a few people, giving them the details of this young man's background and experience, and then asked for a special favor to help him out. To my delight, they agreed that they needed people like him and offered to get him started in a new training program.

You should have seen the light come on in this young man's face, the light of hope as he clung to the belief that something good was going to happen. Given purpose and direction, he became excited about the possibilities he now saw in his life. The transformation was amazing. As I drove him back to the front gate, he leaned over from the back seat and kissed me on the cheek (which is customary over here), thanking me for what I had done for him. He was so appreciative that he could not stop blessing me and my family, my kids, my dogs, and everyone else.

* * *

One of the sources I was working with, Hazam, brought his family from their home south of Baghdad, for the sole purpose of having dinner with Chief Allen, our interpreters, and me that evening. He and his family wanted to show their appreciation for all that we had been doing to help the Iraqi people.

We made our way across the 14th of July Bridge to meet them on the other side, outside of the Green Zone. They were waiting in front of the checkpoint there, ten people crammed into the cab of a small Nissan two-seater pickup, except for Hazam's oldest son, who was sitting in the back with the food.

We motioned for them to follow us as we gained approval from the guards for them to enter the Green Zone. We took them over to the Al-Rasheed Hotel, my late-night disco-dancing location, where we had received permission from the hotel management to have our dinner out by the pool. The Al-Rasheed was Saddam's hotel, being the closest one to his government buildings. It was a high-class hotel built by a Swiss company to provide plush accommodations for Saddam's visitors.

The pale blue pool was large, surrounded by an open area with plenty of white metal pool furniture for us to have our dinner on. It was completely unoccupied, but gave a sense of opulence in its grand size. A massive rectangle, it was three feet deep at one end and 15 feet deep at the other end where the diving platform was. A long bar served a variety of cocktails, sodas, and snacks, making it the perfect place for our gathering.

September meant the worst of the heat had passed and a slight breeze provided the perfect ambiance for a dinner together. Date-palm trees swayed in the evening air and many large shrubs, which hid us from any outsiders, surrounded the pool area.

Hazam's family was beautiful—he and his wife, their children (ranging in age from nine to sixteen), his mother-in-law, his sister-in-law, and his brother-in-law's wife with her three-year-old daughter. What a wonderful Iraqi family—intelligent, well mannered, neatly dressed, and full of optimism. All of them spoke enough English to introduce themselves and even understand some of what we were saying, although we had Russell, my interpreter, and Linda, three of our other interpreters, just in case. We had a wonderful evening under the stars with delicious food and good friends.

About a week after our dinner, I met with Hazam and was saddened to discover there had been an attempt to kill him on his way to our office. There was a contract out on him due to his efforts to take down some of the anti-Coalition organizers in his area. It really disturbed me to learn of the risk he was incurring and the danger of his travels. I offered to give him more firepower if we could just get a weapons permit for him. This would put the odds more in his favor.

As we finished up our meeting, the sun was setting and I was quite concerned about Hazam's welfare, especially after having met his family and his beautiful children. I warned him to be careful, even coaxing him to stay the night in Baghdad so as to not make the treacherous journey to his house at night. He declined and ventured out past the border of the Green Zone unprotected.

I was relieved a few days later to learn Hazam had made it home safely that night and that subsequently his would-be killers had been arrested.

CHAPTER NINE

MONKEY MAGIC

I t was business as usual as I went to meet a new contact at the north gate of the Green Zone. While examining the crowd that morning, I heard an unusual sound. At least it was unusual for that part of town.

There was a child crying somewhere behind the barbed wire that separated us from the throngs of people waiting for their chance to speak with someone. I scanned across the human ocean to see where the crying noise was coming from. The people that lined up each day normally had some civil matter that needed to be settled, so the crowd was almost exclusively male. Occasionally there would be a woman, but almost never a child. I was naturally curious, especially as the sound persisted.

Finally I located her—a young girl, maybe seven years old, separated from her mother and swallowed up by the crowd. But where was her mother? Visitors are granted permission to enter the secured area one at a time, and only the first few had entered. I turned and saw a middle-aged Iraqi woman hobbling on crutches with only one leg. She had apparently left her young daughter outside to wait. The little girl was understandably frightened.

Once I spotted her trembling, scrawny frame, I quickly instructed the MPs to move the barbed wire back to let her join her mother. Her crying stopped as she darted to grab hold of her mother's long black dishdasha, torn and frayed from years of use. As she clung tightly to her mother's dress, I moved over slowly to brush her dark hair away from her eyes and to pat her gently on the head.

Her poverty was painfully evident as I surveyed her tattered dress and worn-out plastic flip-flops. Her tangled black hair was matted against her head, indicating she had not had a bath in some time. Her skin was cracked and blistered from exposure to the scorching sun and constant wind. Tear tracks were visible on her dirty face.

As I crouched down to look into her eyes, a lump got caught in my throat. What could I possibly do to relieve this child's suffering? Then I remembered a box of goodies back in my office that might be just the ticket for this little girl.

I asked the guards to hold the girl and her mother there until I returned. Jumping into my SUV, I scrambled back to my office and rummaged through a FedEx box full of toys and trinkets sent by my teammates back home. I grabbed a comb, a brush, a toothbrush, toothpaste, flip-flops, a whistle, and a stuffed monkey whose long arms with Velcro hands could hang around her neck. I dashed out the door, inviting my interpreter to come along.

As I made my way back to the gate, I saw the little girl and her mother waiting patiently. Bending down, I handed her each item with a smile and a brief explanation. As I gave her the toothbrush, I asked her to be sure to brush every day.

Her eyes lit up with delight as I put the monkey's arms over her head. Although she was somewhat shy, having not dealt with an American soldier before, I could see the excitement in her face as her big brown eyes looked up at me. I walked away quickly so as to not bring too much attention to the little girl. This spontaneous gesture had pretty much drained my "treasure chest."

What a moment! I had the chance to influence Iraqis one heart at a time. What might the ripple effect be from my effort to calm the tears of one Iraqi child? I returned to my office to express thanks to my teammates in the United States who had sent the original box of toys. What a truly inspired idea.

I had only one request of them—please send more toys.

* * *

I was abruptly wakened from my restful sleep by the unmistakable crackle and rumble of explosions going off nearby, reminding me of exactly where I was. Awakening to the sound of rocket-propelled grenade explosions is not the best way to begin the day. I soon found out that the Al-Rasheed Hotel, just a few blocks away, had been hit by two rounds. The Al-Rasheed Hotel housed civilian Coalition officials and some US military personnel. It was a symbol of security within the Green Zone. The attack caused minimal damage and no casualties, but it highlighted the vulnerability of even heavily guarded facilities within the Green Zone. I lay in bed for a while, wondering how someone could have gotten so close to the hotel, deep in the heart of a secure area.

After being awakened by explosions, then hammered by a full day of frustrating and rather unproductive interviews, I suspect my patience started to wear thin by late afternoon. My last appointment was at 6:00 p.m. with Hazam, whose family and companionship we enjoyed so much the week before at the Al-Rasheed Hotel. Hazam was accompanied by his boss, who, along with his brother, was a member of the Iraqi Governing Council.

I should have known by the way the meeting started that I was in for a ride. Hazam's boss came out of the chutes with both (figurative) guns blazing as he declared in an agitated voice that I had a trust issue with him. I told him it wasn't that I didn't trust him, but since I had just met him, my trust would grow over time as we worked together. He found that modus operandi insulting.

I told him, "I trust you because of the trust I have for Hazam. If he trusts you, I trust you." I let him know that at some point I would be able to have total trust for him independent of my friend Hazam. He wasn't pleased with my answer, expecting me to trust him unconditionally because of his family lineage and their two-thousand-year-old tribal history.

In the three-hour rant that followed, he disparaged our efforts, saying that nothing was being done to fix Iraq's troubles and that the Coalition was not solving problems fast enough to satisfy him. As I was already weary from the day's activities, my patience began to wane, and my personal defensive measures began to rear up as he raked the Coalition over the coals in a very direct and personal attack.

Here we were putting our lives on the line every day, away from our families for perhaps over a year, making great personal and financial sacrifices so that the people of his country could reap the benefits of freedom for the first time in their lives—and this guy had the nerve to say that we were not doing enough. My blood was now beginning to boil, but I made every effort to maintain my professionalism and calm demeanor.

He persisted with his rambling rebuke, claiming that we were to blame for members of the Governing Council being targeted and even shot at. This was particularly absurd given the fact that the Governing Council represented the new government of Iraq and as such were a threat to all those who were in the old regime.

He grumbled that he and his brother were considering resigning from the council because they lacked faith in the ability of the United States to resolve their problems and be successful in the endeavor. He felt it would be a blemish on their great family tribe if the United States failed.

I was caught off-guard by his tribe-over-nation mentality. He had neither the patience nor the desire to contribute—much less sacrifice —in order to build a free Iraq. He continued to stress that his personal honor was more important than the building of a free Iraq.

At this point, I was appalled and disgusted with his pompous, arrogant attitude. I imagine he was so willing to speak his mind because he had nothing to lose. Hazam, who had remained quiet up to this point, made an attempt to come to my rescue as his boss persisted to pursue his attack on me. But his boss would not hear of it, telling Hazam in Arabic to shut up and to not say another word. I felt sorry for Hazam and could sense the pain and embarrassment he felt from his boss's remarks.

I was losing it fast. I finally had to leave the room to regain my composure. I grabbed my partner, Chief Allen, who just happened to be passing by, and asked that he take my place until I could compose myself.

I returned after a few minutes, attempting to regain control of the conversation, finish up the meeting, and get this arrogant lout out of my office. As he was going to the door, he thrust in his final dagger when he said he was prohibiting Hazam from seeing any of us again until his demands were met. That concerned me, knowing how valuable Hazam's information had been.

As they were all leaving, Hazam slipped me a note saying he would come to my office the next day to discuss what had happened.

When Hazam returned the next day, he was gushing with apologies. He stated repeatedly how his boss had no concept of what was happening and was clueless about the real situation. He wanted nothing to do with his boss and his boss's brother, convinced that they didn't have what was required to lead Iraq. Hazam was leaving them for good, confident that he could find other people who were willing to work with him to make his dreams become a reality.

Knowing he was obtaining his livelihood from his boss, I told Hazam I wanted to make a donation to his cause by giving him a couple hundred dollars, hoping that he would be willing to take the money under the pretense of his building community support for a free Iraq. At this point, my interpreter started to choke up as she attempted to interpret our sincere expressions of friendship for each other.

The following day, Hazam popped in for a moment to drop off two bunches of plastic flowers his daughters had put together in an effort to cheer me up. I was touched by their kind gesture and knew that Hazam had the moral courage to act independently of his boss.

* * *

At times I felt like I was holding a fishing pole with a whale at the other end, running out the line. I woke several times during the night with my mind bouncing around from one pressing issue to the next. I woke with my fishing line racing uncontrollably, fully engaged in the schedule of the day.

In the midst of reeling in this whale, I found respite in being able to provide some assistance to individuals with urgent needs. One afternoon found me in our military hospital taking the young son of one of my sources to be evaluated by a neurosurgeon. The little boy was suffering from a seizure disorder, at least according to the Iraqi doctors. The child's condition had been worsening over the last few days, forcing us to take action and provide additional evaluation to get some type of care for his condition.

I met with the doctors a few days earlier to arrange for the appointment. The doctors were more than willing to help out due to the nature of the circumstances. I was pleased with their attitude, so gracious and eager to be of assistance. The doctor spent over two hours evaluating the little boy's condition, even to the extent of taking a CT scan. They were somewhat limited by the lack of certain equipment, but the doctor's prognosis was favorable, indicating that the condition didn't appear to be epilepsy.

While I was waiting for the doctor to complete his evaluation, I walked outside to get some fresh air. Passing by the young American guard at the front of the hospital, I offered up the customary greeting, "How are you?" Her response caught my attention, compelling me to turn around and sit down next to her. After further inquiry, she broke down and started to cry, expressing how homesick she was.

In an effort to cheer her up I told her I'd return with a box of toys for her to pass out to the children that came to the hospital. Her eyes lit up and she smiled upon hearing my offer. Maybe that would take her mind off her own separation from loved ones.

There are so many opportunities to reach out to those around us, helping them in time of need. If we are paying attention to our surroundings, many opportunities to brighten another's day will come our way, opportunities to bring a little sunshine into what might otherwise be full of gloom and despair. Sometimes it is just a matter of being sensitive to the signals of someone in need whose path we might pass in the course of our busy life.

CHAPTER TEN

CHIEF WIGGLES

Throughout my time in Iraq, I had been keeping a journal of my experiences. Initially, I emailed these journal entries to friends and family. Eventually, a friend suggested that it would be easier to post the notes on the Internet for everyone to see at once. He helped me set up an Internet journal—a "blog" as they are called by web surfers.

For security purposes I needed a pseudonym on my website. The nickname "Wiggles" has followed me off and on since third grade when someone on the playground called me "Pauly-Wolly-Wiggles." Since I was a chief warrant officer (CW), the name "Chief Wiggles" seemed to fit. I titled my blog "Chief Wiggles—Straight From Iraq."

Initially, I was getting ten to fifteen visitors to the site each week—probably just my wife and kids. Then other people started linking to my site and readership began to grow. On a slow news day, when nobody linked to my site, I might have five hundred to eight hundred visitors a day. When major sites linked to my blog, my readership would often exceed ten thousand. On an average day, over two thousand people would visit.

After sharing some toys with the little girl at the palace gate, I posted a request on my website for more toys to replenish my supply and to keep the good work moving forward. I was overwhelmed by the response.

Pretty soon, I was able to turn to my stash of toys any time I had a few spare minutes to head off to a hospital or orphanage as part of my military responsibilities. The toys continued to arrive in my office, and I continued to find children who loved receiving them.

* * *

The number of opportunities that came my way to brighten a child's day amazed me. It seemed as though the more I looked, the more opportunities started to fall right into my lap. Fortunately, I was able to carry on the tradition started down south at the POW camp and make sure that the Good Luck Genie was able to strike again and again.

One day, a young girl about seven years old came in our office with her father. This man was hoping to pass along some vital information to us regarding a variety of things going on in his neighborhood. As the girl hung back in the doorway, sheepishly hiding behind her father's pant leg, I quickly rummaged through my boxes of toy items for something that might bring a smile out on her pretty face. The minute I gave her a green stuffed frog, one sent to me by my buds at FedEx, she lit up like a Christmas light, smiling from ear to ear.

Another time, I had gone out to the front gate to pick up a source who was waiting there to speak with me. Among the people waiting was a man cradling his little boy in his arms, noticeably in anguish. This boy's entire body had obviously been badly burned, his entire skin now scarred and blistered and peeling. As the boy's fingerless limbs attempted to scratch his itching scabs, I hastily asked my interpreter to ask the father to wait there for me. I knew that what the boy needed, more than anything else, was the kind of medical care that most Iraqi facilities could not provide, but I thought that maybe if I could give him something to hold while he waited, it might ease the passing of time. I quickly escorted my source to the office, then returned as soon as I could with a stuffed animal, the very last one I had left from the two boxes of toys I had received just weeks before. But the father and his little boy were nowhere to be seen. Disappointed, I gave the stuffed animal to the young guard at the gate, asking her to give the boy the gift if by chance he returned.

Not all of my Good Luck Genie recipients were as heartbreaking as this one. I had the opportunity to meet an entire family one evening, the family of a man with whom I had been working for some time. This man had four children, ages eight to sixteen years old, each one well groomed, polite, and outwardly affectionate. As

I met these young people, it reminded me of what I was working so hard for, what we were all fighting and dying for. I was thrilled to be able to respond to their warm greetings with small gifts of toys from my generous American benefactors. Meeting this family helped me realign my perspective about my surroundings, refocusing my sense of purpose and meaning.

* * *

I had asked my American friends and readers of my blog for donations to aid the mission of the Good Luck Genies. The response I received was overwhelming! Once the packages started to arrive, the project seemed to swell and take on a life of its own. I cannot begin to tell you how exciting that was for me, once the boxes of toys started coming into my office. Boxes and boxes of the greatest stuff, carefully and thoughtfully selected. It was like Christmas in October for me and my team as we attempted to sort through everything, organizing the items to ensure that the right gifts went to the right kids. It was so much fun going through the boxes, even playing with the toy dinosaurs as I had flashbacks from my own childhood. I was thrilled with the items sent for these kids. I humbly salute all who found it within themselves to sacrifice their own personal wants to send a package of happiness to the children of Iraq.

I took the first toys and school supplies to a family we visited one evening, treasuring each smile and sparkle in the children's eyes as I handed them the specially selected items. For the rest, I had been working hard to establish a few distribution channels to a variety of destinations. Even before the toys arrived, I had spoken with a few doctors who were hooking me up with the children's hospitals in the country. I was working with a group that regularly goes out to about a dozen orphanages around the country, trying to get my toys into their hands, making plans to accompany them on their next outing. I was also working with about a dozen different schools, arranging a way to provide supplies and toys for the children who attended there.

My efforts were greatly helped along by the generosity of big-hearted individuals all over the world. One of my best friends, Gordon Hanks of Bridgepoint Systems, and his family had agreed to assist me in my efforts by offering a warehouse facility back in the

States to store the collected toys. He also offered the use of a truck he had to help move the toys from place to place. Small miracles like this continued to happen as people everywhere caught the vision of what it meant to the children, putting the smiles back on the faces and the twinkle back in the eyes of the Iraqi youth.

* * *

One morning, a local orphanage with about one hundred girls was having a field day at the Babylon Hotel, not far from the CPA palace. I loaded up some of the toys I had collected into one of the twenty-passenger buses, which served the palace compound—buses kindly donated by Saddam Hussein. These buses had been used by Saddam to shuttle government workers around the compound, but they now served the Coalition. I christened the bus "Chief Wiggles' Toy Bus."

It was a great day as our group of volunteers met with the young Iraqi girls who were on a rare field trip away from the orphanage they called home. They were playing in the garden and tennis court areas of the hotel when we pulled up with a busload of items carefully selected for them.

They were ecstatic as they saw us walking in carrying boxes of toys and school supplies and mounds of stuffed animals. You could see the sparkle in their eyes and their grins of anticipation as each of them greeted our volunteers with a confident, "Hello. What is your name?"

Paul with school girls

85

The girls were eager to include us in their games and festivities and grabbed hold of my hands to play their version of ring-around-the-rosy. They sang, chanted, danced, and clapped, but most of all they laughed. It was a full-hearted laugh, indicating that, at least for that moment, they were completely happy.

After spending a couple of hours with the girls, we made our way back into the Green Zone. The bus was empty, but we were full of joy. It was exactly what we had anticipated when I made the initial request for more toys, knowing we had done a good thing, all of us full of the joy that comes from serving someone else. I was so grateful for the chance to bring happiness to the children of Iraq, one child at a time, spreading simple joys through toys.

With toys now coming in more regularly, I made a special effort to drop off boxes of toys at the local hospital for the staff to hand out to the outpatients. I also made sure that some of our more home-sick soldiers were given boxes of toys, along with the instructions to distribute them when the opportunity presented itself. For me, the toys were a nice diversion from the non-stop talk of crime and violence that filled my working days, and I sensed that they sometimes offered more joy and hope to the givers than perhaps they did to the receivers.

Along with distributing the toys, my team and I were involved in helping people in a variety of ways. Along with doing our part in passing on actionable intelligence to Special Forces teams and pushing reports up the chain, we were also trying to help the Iraqi people start businesses, which we hoped would create good jobs for people who desperately needed to put food on their tables. We also helped some of our sources find housing, get rewards for the stuff they turned in, fill openings with the ministries, and on and on. The opportunities were endless; there were so many ways to make a difference.

But the icing on the cake came with the news that all fifteen of my Generals from Camp Bucca had been released. It had taken countless hours over five long months and the involvement of numerous high-ranking military officers—including five different US generals—to get these men back home with their families. I was so excited as I imagined the joyous reunions they would have with their loved ones.

CHAPTER ELEVEN

OPERATION GIVE

U nexpectedly, our grass-roots effort to bring hope to the children of Iraq had blown out the military's mail system with so many boxes of toys that they could no longer handle the volume. Each day, the mail van would call ahead alerting me that they had another load of boxes for Chief Wiggles.

Then suddenly, our program to "Share Joys with Toys" received a serious setback. The Army APO mail system decided to clamp down, enforcing their policy forbidding goods to be shipped that were intended to be given to another individual. This policy satisfied an elevated security standard and ensured that the troops didn't get packages from unknown individuals. I actually received a "cease and desist" order specifically prohibiting more toys being sent to me at the palace. I understood the Army's position, but that meant we needed to find a way to continue the flow of toys.

Thankfully, Matt Evans, a Maryland attorney and reader of my blog, came up with a kick-butt solution enabling us to continue to reach out to the Iraqi kids with bundles of happiness. He set up a non-profit 501c3 organization—Operation Give. Volunteers then secured warehouse space on the east coast. Toys were sent to the Operation Give warehouse and then shipped by boat in containers to Iraq through what is called the Civil Military Operation Center (CMOC), who then would arrange for the goods to be moved via the military or private contractors to the final destination.

I was so grateful that volunteers in the United States had figured out a way to keep the flow of toys moving. There were hundreds of unknown angels who played a part in putting this solution together and who donated money to help pay for the cost of moving the containers to their final destination in Baghdad.

Operation Give had been launched.

Once again our team of Chief Wiggles' workers descended on a children's hospital in Baghdad with arms full of toys. Our caravan pulled up to the front of the hotel, accompanied by several doctors from our local military hospital, Iraqi friends, interpreters, reporters from NBC and Associated Press, and our combat camera crew.

After a quick meeting with the hospital administrator, we grabbed a few carts and proceeded to deliver our cargo of delight to the children in the hospital. We went from room to room, stopping at as many beds as we could to inquire about the child's condition and prognosis, while we personally handed out a toy selected just for them. It was an incredible experience.

As we went down each hall and ward of the hospital, a following grew behind us as the word of our arrival spread like wildfire. Unfortunately, due to the sheer number of people, we were unable to deliver toys to every employee or family member who desired something. We were there to make sure each and every sick child got a toy.

At one point, a father whose daughter was dying from leukemia confronted me with a plea for medical treatment, not toys. With intense emotion he explained his need for a medical solution to his daughter's ailment, which a toy would not cure. My heart ached for him as I put my arm around him. I was sorry to say that I only had toys in my bag of tricks.

* * *

A man, who was small in stature but big in courage, came into my office desperately seeking someone to talk to. He was obviously under a great deal of stress and was emotionally distraught.

He began to relay to me his story of how his family's house had just been bombed the night prior, for the second time, due to his involvement with Coalition forces. Over the past several months he had continued to provide us with intelligence regarding underground activities around Baghdad, which had resulted in the discovery of several missiles, numerous bad guys, and many caches of weapons.

He started to divulge additional information about the where-abouts of one of our most wanted individuals. I stopped him mid-sentence to inquire of his family's condition, realizing that they had no safe place to live. I told him that the first priority was to find a safe haven for his family.

It was time for the Good Luck Genie to swing into action. I needed to find this man a place to live with his family somewhere in the Green Zone, which was not going to be easy. There were endless rules and restrictions about getting people into the vacated apart-ments in the area, but I was determined. I knew divine assistance was going to lead the way.

With our interpreter along, the three of us jumped into my vehicle as I drove around the area. Miraculously, we met the right people, we went to the right places, and we found a nice apartment in a complex where Saddam's intelligence officers used to live. Every-thing came together just like I knew it would. When the day was over, all I could do was lie in bed, staring up at the ceiling, and say, "Wow! What a great day!"

* * *

The time had finally arrived for my long-awaited reunion with the freed generals from Camp Bucca—a reunion I had been dream-ing of and talking about for months. There were at least six of them who lived in Baghdad. We had been calling for a few days to set up this reunion in order to give some of them a stipend and for me to receive their résumés for any future positions.

It was so strange to see them waiting at the front palace gate dressed up in their finest attire rather than prison jumpsuits. It seemed like a dream from another life. They looked good—no, they looked great!

We had a wonderful meeting, talking about so many things that had happened since my departure from Camp Bucca and their arrival back home. We shared many memories from the camp. Sur-prisingly, we were able to find humor in many of those experiences. I was so glad to hear they were still our advocates and were hopeful for a bright future with the help of the United States.

Two days later, General Saif and General Matta came by to pick me up for a dinner engagement. Just as we had promised each other at Camp Bucca, we were finally all having dinner at Saif's home with his family. I was so excited to meet his family and share an evening with them. The night was everything I dreamed it would be. The food was delicious, the family was delightful, and the evening was perfect. I relished every minute of it.

I gave General Saif's children a couple of stuffed animals, which they immediately snuggled up to. But what the generals gave me in return was unbelievable. The two generals gave me a letter along with their own personal Medals of Honor they had received directly from Saddam Hussein, for heroic acts of courage performed during their military career. They gave me the actual medals with photos of Saddam pinning it on them.

As I read the letter, looked at the pictures, and felt the medal, I was astonished that they would be willing to give up such a treasured service decoration. Sud-

> Dear Paul Holton,
>
> This is my first medal of Brave at the Iraqi - Iran war (March 14 1984). I wish to give it to you for a great memories, and I appreciate your efforts and your behavior and your spirit. I am a proud of meeting a man like you and to have a friend like you.
>
> I hope our friendship will stay forever. May God bless you and your family.
>
>
> Sincerely
> Iraqi Air ForceGB
> Saif ALuqaidy
> Oct 23 2003

Letter given to Paul by General Saif along with his medals of honor

denly, I realized that they were showing me that they were completely ready for a new Iraq without Saddam Hussein.

The meal was incredible to say the least. We enjoyed the best of Iraqi cuisine: flatbread, biryani, dorma, tabouli, and kabobs. I wasn't sure what some of it was, but it was tasty. We topped it off with a light dessert, fruit, and then some nice chocolates and a few more drinks. We stayed until it was almost dark. Unsure of how safe it would be to drive around at night, we knew we had to return to the Green Zone before it got too late.

* * *

My phone rang early the next day, waking me from a sound sleep. It was my interpreter, informing me that the Al-Rasheed Hotel had been attacked again. This time the attack was a missile barrage from nearly point-blank range that killed an American colonel and wounded eighteen other people. Visiting Deputy Secretary of Defense Paul Wolfowitz went scurrying for safety and was unhurt.

I had been there just a few hours earlier for a late-night swim. My interpreter, an occupant of the hotel, was unharmed. Once again, the security of the Green Zone had been violated. This attack had likely been planned over a two-month period as terrorists had put together an improvised rocket launcher and figured out how to wheel it into the park across the street from the hotel.

Every time I started to feel that things were settling down into some form of normalcy, I was reminded of the stark reality of this place. We were constantly concerned for what might happen at any given moment, knowing we could never let our guard down.

At noon, I dashed out the door as another group of six Camp Bucca generals were scheduled to arrive at the North Gate. As I went through the checkpoint, I noticed out of the corner of my eye that two of our most valuable sources, Qies and Emad, were waiting to see me. I was expecting new information about the location of stockpiles of gold and money. I called up to the office to see if someone else couldn't come down to check Qies and Emad through the gate.

I ran to the North Gate to welcome the six generals. As with the first group of six, they were all dressed up in their finest apparel. They were clean-shaven, except for their mustaches, with fresh haircuts and a noticeably different twinkle in their eyes.

I embraced them one by one, expressing my happiness in seeing them as free men. We joked and laughed and were able to recall a few humorous and lighthearted times at the POW camp.

Other sources had also arrived at the gate mixed in with the group of generals. As I embraced the generals, the others looked in wonderment as if this was the way I greeted all of my sources. I wondered if they, too, were expecting a big hug. Not wanting to leave them out, I complied with their apparent expectation and extended jubilant greetings and hugs to all at the gate.

In my office, the generals and I chatted about life since their release and reviewed what was now going to happen to them. Lieutenant Colonel Sarna, who was partly responsible for rebuilding the new Iraqi military, spoke to them for about an hour, reviewing a variety of issues and anticipating their questions and concerns.

Realizing that most of those men had driven for hours to arrive in Baghdad for this appointment, I decided it might be a good idea to have lunch together over at the freshly bombed Al-Rasheed Hotel, where there was an Iraqi restaurant with a pretty good selection of indigenous cuisine.

With my interpreter, I grabbed buddies Qies and Emad and the six generals, loaded everyone on the Chief Wiggles Toy Bus, and headed over to the restaurant. We had a great meal together, with time to reminisce, talk about their families, and look to the future.

On our return trip back to the North Gate, I told them to take a couple of toys home to their families, since all of them had small children. I always left a few boxes of toys on the bus for such special occasions. The toys were like icing on the cake, really capping off a great reunion. We embraced one last time and said our good-byes, and I wished them well in their new life.

With the generals on their way, I turned my attention to Qies and Emad. They came to me with quite a find, uncovering the location of numerous Iraqi helicopters hidden prior to the war. I immediately went to work to determine what would be required to recover those in a timely fashion, before they were cannibalized by others looking to make a quick buck.

* * *

The sounds of explosions rocking Baghdad were commonplace, both day and night. Each explosion reminded me not only of the dangers that lurked outside the Green Zone but also of our vulnerability within this ring of security.

I spoke with a man who was asleep in the Al-Rasheed Hotel when a rocket-propelled grenade came through his window, slid along the wall, and lodged in his closet full of clothes but fortunately did not explode. He was one lucky guy with only glass cuts on his face from the shattering mirror. Had the grenade exploded, he surely would have been killed.

For a few days, things had been relatively quiet, except for the sound of the occasional barrage of automatic weapon fire, which felt more like background static than anything threatening. I prayed each evening that the night would pass without incident or death.

All of the entranceways to our buildings were guarded by a group of retired Gurkhas from Nepal, known for being some of the best soldiers in the world. They were all very diligent in performing their duties, taking their security jobs seriously. I had found all of them to be courteous and polite. They had taken the time to learn enough English to greet us with the appropriate salutation. I made friends with a number of them that I saw daily and learned how to greet them in Nepali.

As I pulled into the parking lot, the mail truck was waiting for me with another load of about twenty-five boxes of toys for Operation Give. With some help from Qies and Emad, we tossed the boxes onto the bus. I was grateful for another load of toys to distribute.

Along the way, we decided to engage in a Chief Wiggles activity, picking up people along the side of the road who were in need of a ride. We picked up two Iraqis carrying a propane tank and a mother and her children who had just been to the market. I had my interpreter pass out toys to the kids before letting them off at their stops.

Continuing to broaden the scope of toy distribution, I found a way to send toys to places I wouldn't have been able to get to on my own by outfitting two different groups of people with boxes of donated toys and supplies. One group was the civil affairs people from my region, who were going south to visit an orphanage. The other group was people from my office who were accompanying the Governing Council to visit a couple of schools in smaller towns and villages in the north. I loaded both groups up with plenty of toys for their excursions and sent them on their way.

Hope and faith were our best weapons against the constant barrage of negative reports. The media reports of death only showed what was happening on the surface, but they were never able to capture the bigger picture and the inner complexities of our world. Americans could understand body counts and images of destruction. But educating and informing the world about the deep-rooted and centuries-old issues in Iraq and the region was a far more difficult task.

The media shied away from reporting on the multi-layered and complex nature of the region. Perhaps they didn't possess the knowledge and background to understand the situation, or maybe, due to time constraints, they chose to deliver a more superficial view. Regardless, if the American people were better informed of the intricacies of Iraq, they might have a very different perception of the work being done in Iraq and the expected outcomes.

The bottom line was that Iraq is a multifarious, complicated, and messy environment, one that I just barely understood myself. There are myriad cultural, religious, tribal, political, historical, and geographical elements all intertwined into a complex web, intermixed with threads of mysticism and superstition, spun by greed and a continual thirst for power and survival ignited by Saddam himself.

CHAPTER TWELVE

RAMADAN

The pace of life slowed down a bit with the start of Ramadan, the holiest season of the Muslim calendar. For Iraqis, observing the sacred month-long holiday meant ritual fasting, praying, and staying away from earthly pleasures, including smoking, from sunrise to sunset. This was difficult for many of our sources who were chain-smokers. I knew that they were coming in a little on-edge and eager for the sun to go down. As night overtook another day in Baghdad, our sources returned to their homes to celebrate *iftar*, the meal that breaks the fast.

All day long they filled my head full of stories of corruption, murder, deceit, and attacks on Coalition forces. The overload lights finally went off in my head, my mind having been pumped all day with doom and gloom. My negative story meter was way past the maximum level tolerable for any given day. If I heard one more report of dishonesty and scheming, I was going to explode.

The final source of the day nearly lit my fuse. Revealing specific information on corruption within the Governing Council, Iraq's interim governing body, he held back on the real meat unless I met his demands for a car, a phone, and payment for his expenses. I was hoping this Iraqi citizen, out of the goodness of his heart and with a desire to serve his country, would offer up the information that might prove to be invaluable. Instead of reporting corruption, his primary concern was personally profiting from the corruption. Obviously, what I hoped for was not going to happen.

Fortunately, my friends Captain Qies and Captain Emad, the two pilots, showed up, allowing me to release some pressure as we discussed ways of moving toys around the country. I even found a warehouse in the Green Zone to house all of the toys and supplies we were collecting.

Both men were extremely eager and willing to help in any way they could. Aside from being great sources (having shared valuable intel with us on numerous occasions), they were honest God-fearing men who loved their families and their country, men of like mind and heart who shared my vision and understood what I was attempting to accomplish.

Captain Emad had been to flight school in the United States, had traveled abroad on numerous occasions prior to Saddam taking power, and spoke English quite well. Captain Qies—a soft-spoken, gentle man, somewhat shy about speaking English—was always there to lend a helping hand. These two men were inseparable; they always showed up together, full of ideas, new intel, and a strong, driving desire to be part of my operation.

With these two men, my interpreter, Dr. Eaman (whom I will talk about later), and of course Conan—better known as "Baghdaddy"—acting as my personal bodyguard, we had the start of the Operation Give team. And we finally even had a place to store the hundreds of boxes sent to us by caring, generous Americans. In what appeared to be an abandoned garage, surrounded by US tanks and Bradleys (apparently guarding our stash of donated toys), we sorted and stacked the boxes ready for future deliveries. The pieces were all falling into place, creating the perfect storm for Operation Give to take advantage of.

As we were transporting toys to the warehouse, we were able to hand out some to children in the Green Zone, who were often out playing in the streets. I pulled the bus into one of the neighborhoods, stopping at the sight of the first child on the side of the road. Within a few minutes, we had fifty children gathered around the bus as we passed out items through the windows to the outstretched hands of the children below.

The children were climbing all over the bus. Several were able to stand on the tires and put their faces up to the level of my window in

Passing out toys from Chief Wiggles' Toy Bus to eager children

the driver's seat. I made them ask politely, saying "please" and "thank you" as I passed out stuffed animals and toys. Patting their heads, pinching their cheeks, and handing out treats was a pleasant diversion from the soul-grinding task of military debriefing.

A few days later, we gathered in the parking lot at our scheduled time, preparing to depart for another outing for "Sharing Joys with Toys." The bus was overflowing with toys; I felt like I was driving Santa's sleigh. Organizing the convoy was critical, with the Chief Wiggles Toy Bus sandwiched between two Humvees for protection. With loaded weapons across our laps, we took off for a handicapped children's hospital, completely unaware of what we were going to find awaiting us.

We made a quick stop by the Green Zone Army hospital to pick up a few doctors, both American and Iraqi. They wanted to share in the experience of passing out toys. As usual, Captain Qies and Captain Emad and Ali were there to offer their assistance, having been with us on most of the other toy outings. It was essential to have Iraqis with us that could speak both Arabic and English. Emad brought his teenage daughter along to be part of the team.

As we pulled up to the back gate of the "hospital," we discovered it was actually more of a care facility or asylum. The workers and children were busily preparing for our arrival, washing and sweeping the area. Some children were already out in their wheelchairs to

97

offer up an enthusiastic welcome, and we were greeted warmly by the director of the facility.

It was immediately apparent that things were very difficult for the children at this facility. As I looked through the bus windshield, I noticed one child sitting on the ground with swarms of flies buzzing around her head and face.

We stepped off the bus into the hospital's open courtyard, which had just been hosed down, but we could still smell and see the unsanitary conditions. I had never seen such a run-down place for handicapped children before. Most of the children appeared to be mentally handicapped and suffering from motor-skill impairments.

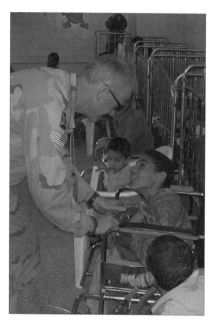

Chief Wiggles (Paul) with children at handicapped hospital

Over the next hour, we made our way through the rooms full of children and young adults, passing out carefully selected toys, hoping to bring joy to an otherwise neglected group of children. We handed out balls to those that could play with them, along with Tonka trucks and toy cars to boys who immediately began pushing them along the ground. Stuffed animals were given to all the young girls, who snuggled them as tightly as they could.

It was heart-wrenching to say the least. All of us were deeply saddened by the tenement-like circumstances. It was difficult to see, yet rewarding, as the children responded so warmly. However, Emad's daughter had to return to the bus to wait; she simply wasn't able to handle the deplorable conditions.

Doctor Eaman, an Iraqi medical doctor who frequented the hospital, mentioned that conditions had actually improved over the last few months. They had cleaned up the facility and changed the way the children were cared for. It was hard to imagine how awful it must have been before the upgrades. They went out of their way to show us a storage room that had been converted into a cafeteria. We were shown another room, which had been made into a usable playroom. This enabled the children to be taken out of their rooms during the day. The surroundings were bleak for these forgotten children.

The hospital director was appreciative of our efforts to help these children have a few moments of recreation. She mentioned other such facilities around the country with even worse conditions, which were desperately in need of our assistance. It was painful to think that what she said might be true.

I was aware that, in addition to toys, many Americans had made cash donations on Operation Give's website. I promised to assist in making some facility improvements and vowed to work with the hospital director in any way I could. I offered to put a padded play mat in the playroom so that the children wouldn't have to play on the cold cement floor.

As we drove away, I thought what a great experience it was and how we had made a difference with something as small and simple as a toy.

* * *

As I worked away in my office one night, the sound of incoming mortar rounds drove me into the palace's basement to seek refuge. It wasn't particularly frightening, but the enemy's increasing luck or improving accuracy was a little unnerving. Several of the rounds found cars in the parking lot nearby as their target. Fortunately, no one was hurt as a result of these explosions, but we were all a bit rattled.

The next night, in anticipation of additional incoming rounds and hoping to lighten up the situation, I made a little wager with the guards at the palace's front gate concerning what time we would hear the incoming rounds that night. Each of us picked a time and threw a couple of bucks into the kitty.

At my selected time I began hearing a string of explosions but realized quickly they weren't incoming but outgoing. It sounded as if we were really stirring up somebody's life. I wasn't exactly sure what it was, but it sounded like tanks and helicopters were involved. It went on for several minutes, one explosion after another. Knowing that we were taking action, I found those sounds of return fire especially encouraging. That was a wager I was happy to lose.

The enemy mortar fire, return fire, and organized enemy attacks continued. One night after returning from appointments, I received a call from one of my sources, who informed me that he could see someone launching mortars in front of his house. He reported that this terrorist was driving up and down the street, stopping just long enough to launch a couple of rounds. Hearing that news, I went over to the Joint Operation Center (JOC) to inform them of this activity, confident that one of the Special Forces teams could stop this one-man rampage immediately.

It wasn't only the incoming fire that kept us on our toes; it seemed that everything was constantly changing around us. One night while out at one of the gates, I came across a family trying to get in to visit a family member hospitalized at the Green Zone facility. The guards were not able to allow them entrance, so I agreed to carry in the sack of food they had prepared, after checking the contents thoroughly. I had a couple of stops to make before arriving at the hospital, but I finally made it to my destination with the sack of goodies, only to find that the patient had been transferred to another hospital outside of my area. I left the sack anyway, hoping the hospital might be able to send the food over with another runner.

It was the continual newness of life in Iraq, the constant change brought about by the evolution of variables in and out of my control, which kept my time there so exciting and meaningful. Everything was in a state of flux; there was no such thing as status quo. Each day's unpredictability made waking in the morning such a treat. Change was the only constant. I woke each day without any idea of what might happen or what new thing might fall into my lap.

* * *

In the course of my discussions with numerous sources, I continued to hear the word *jinn*, or genie, brought up as Iraqis discussed the supernatural powers of Saddam and his followers. I figured that the word meant something quite different than the

Good Luck Genie I had played back in Camp Bucca, but I didn't know just how deeply this legend had taken root in the people of Iraq. Even the most educated of Iraqi sources, which I would have expected to be more sensible, believed in the powers of the genie tribes. Their belief system acknowledged a separate realm, or spirit world, referred to as the "genie world," which consisted of different-colored genie tribes. Saddam was supposedly in charge of the Red Genie Tribe and, as their master, he could command the forces of the genies as he willed.

Out of curiosity for what was behind this belief, I began to ask sources if they had ever seen or had any dealings with a genie. I was surprised by the answers I received and the extent of their belief in the world of the genies, which are described in the Quran as "spirits of evil."

There were so many supposed eyewitness accounts and genie sightings that I began having them describe what they saw, while our artist/interpreter listened and illustrated what they said. I ended up with quite a collection of stories and drawings of monster-like creatures, half human and half animal, with mixed animal parts.

One day, Yousef, one of our sources, brought with him a man who claimed to be the Green Genie Tribe Master. Yousef said he was going to use the Green Genie Tribe Master to help us find Saddam Hussein. As he closed the drapes of the room and laid down enough cardboard for all of us to sit down, he motioned for us to take off our shoes and sit in a circle.

For what seemed like an eternity, we sat listening to the Genie Master acting as the medium for the genies to speak to us. He spoke using a different voice, as if the genie were speaking through him. After listening to all kinds of gibberish and strange tales of seemingly inconceivable things, we couldn't help but be somewhat skeptical; at times we had to work to hold back laughter.

Then, all of a sudden, the Genie Master jumped to his feet while informing us that the Red Genies were coming and they needed to leave the building immediately. Within a few seconds all of them were standing, had put their shoes on, and were running down the corridors of the palace in an attempt to get to their cars before the genies arrived.

It was quite a sight to behold—grown men in suits running for their lives from these invisible but powerful genies. That was the last time we heard from the Genie Master, and nothing ever came of any of the marvelous insights gleaned from the Genie Master's séance.

* * *

Work in the CPA palace, especially in our office, was a hectic, unpredictable, bizarre pressure cooker. Initially, it was just Chief Allen and I on this elite team of military debriefers. About a month later, we were joined by Specialist Conan "whosyourbaghdaddy" Heimdal, a friend from days at Camp Udairi. The final addition was Sergeant Charm. The four of us constituted the only team of its kind in the palace. If you were an Iraqi with some important information to share with the Coalition—if you knew the whereabouts of weapons, bombs, insurgents, land mines, money, or persons of interest, and wanted to give that information to the highest level in the country—we were your first line of contact.

With such a critical mission, it was important for members of our team to stay well connected with each other. Although we had separate vehicles and were often spread out on assignments all over the area, we were in constant contact with each other, particularly by cell phone. For both security and success, we had to work closely together. We learned to play to each other's strengths and cover each other's weaknesses.

Each team member brought different skills and abilities that we weaved into a system that worked well and kept us going day after day. Chief Allen was particularly good at working with tribal leaders and in working with Russell, one of our expert interpreters. Debriefing tribal leaders required the ability to work effectively with competing factions and the complex politics of these groups. Chief Allen and Russell were well versed in US strategies for dealing with these men and their bickering contingents. As the third man, Baghdaddy often was forced to play "clean up," handling the most obnoxious or annoying sources who were just looking for a job, money, or some other favor. Sergeant Charm, the new kid on the block, rounded out the team with his remarkable sense of humor and edgy originality. Laughter became the superglue for our team.

Some sources just dropped in at one of the Green Zone gates throughout the day, while others were brought in by nationals working in the palace. There was no telling how many sources we would be dealing with at any given time, and there was no way to schedule or manage the flow. Dealing with such a high volume of Iraqi sources, all with unfamiliar and seemingly similar names, we were forced to come up with creative ways to keep them all straight. We gave many of them code names, partly for confidentiality and partly to bring some fun to this intense kind of work. There was "Fat Tony," "The Snake Charmer," "Stinkypants," and many others. We even had an in-house caricaturist who would draw spontaneous cartoons poking fun at some of the more bizarre characters.

No question about it, we were loose cannons—but only in a good sense. To a certain degree, we ran our own show and had free rein. We were given a clearly defined mission, then cut a wide berth in what we could do, say, offer, and promise to sources. Our commanding officers weren't in our building, nor did we have daily contact with them. With this kind of relaxed leadership, we became experts at instant improvising, creative problem-solving, and devising off-the-wall workable solutions to our daily dilemmas—while not having to get approval for every move like some rookie salesman on a used car lot.

Strangely, many of the people working at the CPA palace could spend their entire tour there and never meet an Iraqi face to face. It was secluded, well guarded, and highly secure—a totally American compound in the heart of Baghdad, with more acreage than Central Park.

In contrast, the nature of our position put us in continuous daily interaction with Iraqis at every level of the social, professional, political, and military hierarchy. Learning how to effectively deal with them and gain their trust was our constant challenge.

There was always a lot going on in our office, demanding different resources, strategies, and skills. We were family that looked out for and took care of each other. To remain successful, safe, and sane, we were always watching each other's backs, filling in for each other, and pulling up the slack from time to time. We were tightly bound together by an unspoken creed.

My favorite relief from the daily stress came from planning and executing our toy deliveries for Operation Give. A new shipment of cuddly stuffed animals could resuscitate the most miserable problem-choked day. Receiving a phone call from the mail van announcing a delivery from the States would brighten up the day for all of us. With minimal resources, we developed an incredibly efficient system. Whichever team member was available would receive the shipment, transfer the boxes from the mail van to the toy bus, and then move the toys directly to the warehouse. Minimum effort and maximum result.

* * *

One day, when I was behind the wheel of the Chief Wiggles Toy Bus, I found myself in an area of the Green Zone where I hadn't spent much time before. I pulled the bus up to the side of the road when I saw a few kids playing in a pile of rubble behind some bombed-out buildings. I had a few toys in the back, as I usually did, in anticipation of seeing children. My interpreter knew what was going on, and she quickly dashed to the back of the bus to grab a few stuffed animals. She was the first one out of the bus handing out the stuffed animals to the little girls that had gathered. Seeing a couple of boys, I went back to snag a few toy cars for them.

These kids were extremely poor, with their shredded and stained clothes and shoeless feet. Their skin was cracked from the extremes of the weather, their faces dirty from not bathing, and their hair tangled and stringy. The only toys in sight were the broken bricks of the demolished building they were playing in.

Pulling the toy cars from behind my back where I had hidden them, I handed one to the littlest boy in the group. As he looked down at the toy car in his hands, his eyes opened as big as two silver dollars and his mouth dropped wide open. Then a huge smile came across his whole face, responding as if he had never held a toy before. No words were spoken or necessary; his face fully expressed his appreciation for the moment. My only regret was that I didn't have my camera to capture it. Those expressions of joy never became routine or commonplace. Each new experience was exciting, fresh, and totally satisfying.

* * *

We can make a difference in another person's life in any situation we find ourselves in, sometimes by the most seemingly insignificant acts of kindness. No matter where we were or where we went, there were so many opportunities to share something with others, making a lasting impression on everyone we touched. There was always a way to have a Good Luck Genie moment as we hustled around in our daily life, even when we thought we were too busy.

One day, I was driving back from the North Gate in my bus when I passed by a couple of guys walking along the side of the road. Spotting them a bit too late to stop, I turned the bus around and went back to see if they needed a lift. They jumped aboard, indicating that they were going my way. When they saw the stuffed animals I kept on the dashboard of my bus, (so the kids would know it was me when I pulled up), one of the men told me about his two kids at home. As we approached their stop, I willingly handed over two of the toys for his children. He was so excited to have received the animals that as he left the bus he could not stop thanking me for my generosity, commenting that if the Iraqi people really knew what the Americans were like they would change their attitudes and be more willing to cooperate with us in all that we are doing.

In a hundred ways, the "Sharing Joys with Toys" campaign gave me a diversion from the negative to enjoy moments of true happiness as I traveled around passing out toys to any young ones I spotted. It was truly a miraculous thing to watch the joy and happiness on their young faces as they received a small gift of love. Perhaps this was the first such toy in their young lives, having been deprived from even having toys by a regime that had done everything to neglect them.

I was working with several Iraqi nationals (mainly Dr. Eaman, Qies, and Emad) to continue the efforts of Operation Give in Iraq after I left, which was scheduled for sometime in March. I hand-selected these people who I knew and trusted to continue to make this happen. These individuals had already proven themselves by participating in many toy drops to locations all over the country. We were able to reach small towns and villages in areas that otherwise would have never been able to see a toy. We visited hospitals, orphanages, schools, neighborhoods, and children all over the country.

I kept Dr. Eaman busy setting up visits to orphanages and homes, especially those with handicapped children or those who were deaf or blind. This amazing doctor has dedicated so much of her own personal time and resources, free of charge, to ensure the well-being and proper care of Iraqi children, and she continues to be an inspiration to me.

Boxes of toys continued to trickle in, even long after the APO mail system shut us down, at the rate of about ten boxes a day. We now had over one thousand boxes received through the APO system, which was incredibly fantastic. Plus we continued to receive so many more packages at our location in Baltimore, filling up a forty-foot container full of toys.

* * *

As Ramadan came to an end, the fasting gave way to feasting. Eid is a three-day holiday of feasting and gift-giving at the conclusion of Ramadan. During this time, it's customary for families to travel around to friends and relatives, sharing meals and giving gifts.

If someone drops in with their children during Eid, you're expected to have gifts, money, or both for the little ones. Several of our important sources brought their children over to meet me, which gave me an opportunity to give toys from America to the children and to solidify our relationship with their parents.

I got a call from the North Gate from a source named Mohammed. He had come with his kids to introduce them to me. I was happy to oblige. As I slipped out the door, I quickly made a stop at the warehouse to pick up a few toys. He had a beautiful young daughter and cute twin boys.

I put together a small box of school supplies, stuffed animals, small toy cars, and special items I thought each would like, with a couple of new toothbrushes and toothpaste to top it off. I pulled up in the toy bus and motioned for them to jump in. Mohammed gathered the kids and pushed them inside, and I drove over to a quiet spot out of traffic.

The children were quiet, not really sure about how to act around an American, especially an American soldier with full army gear and a loaded weapon in his lap. They were all dressed up in their finest clothes, nicely groomed, obviously cleaned up for the occasion. They were beautiful kids, evidently taking after their mother, who wasn't able to make the trip.

I placed the box on my lap and took out each item, handing them to the intended child, whose eyes opened wide in anticipation. They were appreciative and well-mannered as they offered up a sincere "Thank you very much" in Arabic.

There were always toys on hand to entertain
the children who came to visit at the CPA

I first met Mohammed a couple months prior under very different circumstances. He appeared at the North Gate and told the guards that he had some valuable information, which he desired to pass along to someone. I took the call and told the guard I would be out at the gate to pick him up momentarily.

When I arrived at the gate with an interpreter, I saw Mohammed, a tall, skinny, Iraqi man in his late thirties. He seemed somewhat nervous and uneasy. I broke the ice by introducing myself as the CPA's debriefer and told him I would be more than happy to speak with him about his information.

He was comparatively well-dressed, in a suit and tie, which struck me as odd considering the attire worn by most of my sources. He was clean-cut and freshly shaven. He spoke a small amount of

English, attempting to initially talk to me on his own without the use of my interpreter. He seemed unsure about what he was doing, but pressed on nonetheless.

In his quiet, humble way, he told me about a number of illegal activities he had witnessed firsthand, but the one thing that stuck out in my mind was his story about a counterfeiting operation going on in Baghdad. He seemed to have explicit details about this operation, saying that he used to work for the man who was in charge. He knew everything about what, where, when, and how this counterfeiting ring had been and was operating.

After having worked as a debriefer for only a couple of months, I had already become quite cynical. I was getting tired of listening to so many rumors of operations and activities that never panned out. But this one seemed different. The amount of detail was surprising, giving him significant credibility. He claimed to have been there and seen the operation with his own eyes. He drew me a map of the area, named the streets, and gave me the layout of the counterfeiters' premises.

I told him our next step was to get one of our action teams, a Special Forces team, to go with him to scope out the area. I asked him if he would be willing to travel with the team to identify the location and the specific buildings involved. He said he would, but only if we provided some type of cover or disguise.

The next couple of months were full of frustration as I tried to entice any of our teams to pick up the lead and make the initial recon of the area, in hopes that they would then conduct the raid and take down the criminals. To my dismay and disappointment, I could not get any takers. Even after discussing the details with various groups, I was turned down flatly each time with the excuse that they were too busy or were focusing on more important targets.

After each attempt to persuade someone to take the bait and turn Mohammed's information to action, my source became more and more discouraged with my lack of results, wishing at times that he had not come forward with the information. He had taken a great amount of risk in coming to talk to me, especially since he was quite close to the kingpin. He was concerned about his wife and small children, knowing that we would not be able to protect him from any retaliation.

I finally realized I was not going to be able to facilitate any type of action against these criminals through normal channels and decided I needed to take another course of action. After serious reflection on the matter, I decided to hand the case over to a team of policemen from Hella, a suburb of Baghdad, who were working with the Governing Council. I had worked with the Hella police chief for some time and knew his allegiance to our cause. I set up an appointment to introduce Mohammed and his evidence to this group to take action.

They did their initial drive-by to survey the area, came up with a game plan, and selected a day for it to go down. Everything seemed ready to go, with the Hella police ready for any and all contingencies, or so it seemed.

On the night of the scheduled raid, the Hella policemen conducted their surprise attack on the counterfeiting gang at the designated location just as planned. But they did not expect the Baghdad police to show up at the appointed time to supposedly assist in the operation. Once the doors were opened and several hundred satellite dishes were discovered on the scene, the Baghdad police were so busy trying to steal or hide the dishes for themselves that the whole operation became chaotic and unruly and was nearly a disaster.

The leader of the Hella policemen frantically called me that night in my office to see if I could solicit the help of the American MPs in the vicinity to secure the area. I immediately complied with his request, mainly to prevent the Baghdad policemen from stealing the evidence. With the help of the MPs in the immediate vicinity, several criminals were arrested, bags and bags of evidence were confiscated, and the printing presses were destroyed. They seized the plates, negatives, and the equivalent of several million dollars in Iraqi counterfeit currency.

Surprisingly, the counterfeiting operation was producing both the old and the new Iraqi currency, suggesting that the operation had been up and running long before the start of the war. We were also surprised that the operation was producing the new currency at least two weeks before it was to be officially released for distribution in Iraq. There was also evidence at the scene that led us to believe that the operation had connections to Saddam's sons and links to organizations in other countries.

Left: Iraqi counterfeiter is captured with a box of fake currency
Right: Printing press used by counterfeiters

The bust was a very successful operation and a triumph for all those involved. All the evidence was taken the next day over to the Iraqi Governing Council to be put on display and filmed by several news crews. This was big news and made the headlines of the morning paper.

But the real story was what transpired next. After the criminals had been in jail in Hella for a week or so, they were inexplicably transferred over to the Karada police station in Baghdad. We then heard stories from policemen at that station that a police division head, Chief Ahmed, had his driver showing up on a daily basis with food and comfort items for the prisoners.

Within a matter of days after they had been jailed in Baghdad, the prisoners were, to our total disappointment, released by the judge and the policemen at that station. I was outraged, feeling discouraged for trying to make a difference only to be thwarted by the police and the judge. No sooner did we get the counterfeiters behind bars than they were released by a corrupt system that was supposed to be upholding and enforcing the law.

At that point, I was determined to get to the bottom of this case, to find out who was involved in the counterfeiters' release and why. I began gathering information about the policemen at the Karada station and about the judge who allowed them to flee. At every turn it became evident that the police and the judge had been paid off. All the evidence led back to Chief Ahmed.

Once the word got out at the CPA that I was working on the corruption of the police and the judicial system, other people at the CPA—including the Ministry of Interior, their own internal affairs staff, and the Ministry of Justice—began coming to my office to collaborate with me on this case. They had also started their own investigation of the police and the Ministry of Justice to uncover and eliminate any type of corruption in the ranks of the judicial and law enforcement systems.

We began having regular meetings to share information and to coordinate our efforts to determine the scope and depth of the problem. Both the Ministry of Interior and the Ministry of Justice began turning over sources to me for debriefing, individuals who claimed to have had firsthand knowledge of corrupt activities being conducted by the police. I personally met with numerous sources who were victimized by the Iraqi police. Case after case cited the mismanagement of evidence, theft, corruption, and bribery, all of which seemed to lead to the top and to Chief Ahmed.

I was beginning to have quite a large file on their corrupt activities, even getting direct information from former policemen who were aware of the workings of the police department. One former policeman brought me several citizens who had been victimized, relating to me independently the sad details of their encounter with the police.

One evening, the head of the Iraqi Internal Affairs department took me over to the home of the Iraqi Minister of Interior to have a late-night discussion. The Minister informed me of a vote that was going to be taking place the next morning by the Governing Council to elect Chief Ahmed to the position of deputy minister, further empowering him with more control and additional potential for corruption.

As I heard about this election, I felt I needed to do whatever I could to make key persons aware of the case I had been building against Chief Ahmed. I felt an urgency to inform those in positions of power and control to consider the evidence against him before making their decision. My heart and my mind compelled me to act, to do something, to make others aware of the potential dangers of the Governing Council's impending actions.

With the words of the Minister still ringing in my head, I raced back to my office to write several letters to Ambassador Bremer's office, to the Governing Council, and to my own chain of command, to make sure they all knew what was going on. I sent emails to those in command so they would know what I'd done and be able to act promptly. This was serious. Something needed to happen immediately.

About 7:45 a.m., before there was much activity in the compound, I discreetly dropped off a letter to the ambassador and to the Governing Council outlining the information that I had collected, hoping for a speedy response to this potentially inflammatory intelligence.

Almost immediately, I received a call from Ambassador Bremer's office. Instead of interest in the issues I was presenting, I was peppered with questions regarding the whereabouts of the letter I had written to the Governing Council. The executive assistant to the ambassador did not hide her irritation in her sharp command.

"Retrieve it immediately."

I wanted to explain my position, to discuss the situation, to consider options, but this was the Army. I heard myself snap an immediate, "Yes, ma'am," as I jumped into action.

Fortunately, I knew exactly where I had placed the letter that morning. It was clearly addressed to the head of the Governing Council, Adnan Pachachi, placed in a manila folder, and prominently left for his scheduled arrival. But over half an hour had passed, and I started to panic thinking that maybe it had already been opened. If so, I was doomed.

Dashing back to the Governing Council's office, I held my breath as I turned the corner. The meeting the letter was intended for was scheduled to start in a few minutes. Surely, it would be gone.

But there it was. Still in its place, in the folder where I had left it, seemingly untouched. I snatched it quickly and darted back to my office. I arrived trembling but grateful.

I never did hear back from anyone in my chain of command regarding the contents of the letter, leaving me somewhat dismayed by the whole experience. I had been told that my mission was to gather information of a critical nature and push it to action in a timely fashion. I was unable to do so in this case, watching it end suddenly and without results.

No one in the ambassador's office ever explained what I did wrong or what they were concerned about, but the letter hung over me like a dark cloud for the remainder of my tour in Iraq.

In the course of further investigation, I discovered that the judge had released the prisoners due to "lack of evidence," even though the judge himself had signed a receipt for the very evidence he was claiming did not exist. I saw the receipt and a list of the evidence that was turned in at the time of the counterfeiting operation raid. It was clear that the judge had been paid off or blackmailed to ignore the evidence. The judge was later removed from office after I turned the file over to the Ministry of Justice.

CHAPTER THIRTEEN

A DAY AT SCHOOL

One afternoon, as part of the "Share Joys with Toys" campaign, my team went to the Green Zone Community Center, which housed a girls' primary school. We passed out toys and school supplies, all made possible by generous Americans from the other side of the world. Getting out into the community and sharing the bounty of so much kindness was always the high point of the week.

For the most part, the abandoned homes of the former regime employees in the Green Zone were left in pretty bad condition after having been destroyed or totally ransacked of every possible thing of value. Many of the families who moved into the area were destitute and were little more than squatters in the neighborhood.

The school itself was totally run-down, having been neglected for years. Education was not a priority for Saddam's repressive regime. The poorly lit schoolroom was an eyesore: paint peeling, desks cracked, chairs dilapidated, and walls barren. There was absolutely nothing fun or interesting like you would normally expect in an elementary school.

But the kids were great. The young ladies were so well-behaved and well-mannered, all sitting patiently in their chairs, quick to respond in unison with a loud, rehearsed, "Good morning," in English. They looked beautiful, with smiles that were tempered with a certain shyness typical of Iraqi girls, who are hesitant to respond even when prompted to do so.

We went from room to room with boxes of toys, making sure that everyone received something to brighten their day. We passed out combs and hairbrushes, pencils and pens, dolls and stuffed animals. The gifts were ideal for these girls, appreciation beaming from their faces.

We sat down with them in their little chairs and desks. It was a tight fit, but it made them laugh. I bumbled my way through a few words I had learned in Arabic. It was great to hear their laughter and to see their smiles. They were all so beautiful.

Children in the schoolroom

I saved a few of the best toys for last, not sure how to give out a few special items to a classroom of girls. I decided to have a little quiz to see who was keeping up on current events. I stood in front of the class with my interpreter and instructed them to raise their hand if they knew the answer. I requested they not blurt out the answer and told them we would select the first hand raised.

I asked, "Who is the President of the United States?" They all blurted out, "Bush." With no way to select a winner for that round, I had to go with more difficult questions like, "What is the capital of the United States?" and "What is the population of Iraq?"

As their little hands quickly popped up, the first hand was chosen and the special toys were handed out to the delighted winners. It was a great experience for the team and the news crew that had tagged along. Surprisingly, the girls all had a basic knowledge of English, but were for the most part just too shy to use it, unless prodded to do so by a pushy schoolteacher. Even so, they never missed a chance to say "Hello" and "Thank you".

Having visited a number of boy schools also, there was a stark contract between the boys and girls schools. Perhaps as one would expect even in America, the girls were much more orderly and well-behaved, displaying more self-constraint even when it meant getting a nice new toy. I am sure it had a lot to do with their culture and religion, but I enjoyed it all the same, relishing in the fact that we could actually hand out toys to every student, without having to be concerned about some kid running off with our stash.

With their clothes torn and tattered, the children were obviously from some of the poorest of families. I am sure they were just happy to be able to go to some kind of school. And for a change they were on the receiving end of a few very nice new toys.

It was strange to be in an elementary school, a place for young kids to learn, with no colored pictures on the walls but plenty of graphic depictions of war and the military. Weapons and soldiers decorated their walls, giving a twisted idea of what children that age should be learning. It was appalling to see the remnants of the old regime still casting its shadow on the educational system. One dramatic change had occurred, though—Saddam's picture, once in the front of every book, was now noticeably missing.

In the drab, colorless surroundings of their school, it was as if someone had taken out the normally cheerful elementary school's soul. The bright colors you would expect adorning the walls were replaced with a dark, dreary gray, perhaps indicative of the hopes of these children. Neglected and forgotten by a power-crazed government, these children lived with few expectations for the future, but perhaps we could change all of that. Perhaps in our own little way, through our small acts of kindness, we could put light and color back into the eyes of the children we came in contact with.

* * *

One day to the next usually showed the huge contrast between the highs of spreading joy to the nightmares of war. I'd had a day of emergencies to handle, each one as important as the next, urgent situations stemming from the corruption that had already crept into several of the new government organizations. There seemed to be no end to the Saddam wannabes in this country, making the selection process that much more difficult and critical.

One of my sources discovered, defused, and brought to me two bombs that had been planted under bridges outside of Baghdad. They were intended to kill American troops traveling through the area. As a result of this type of information, we were making significant progress: people were arrested, weapons were found, bombs were defused, groups were broken up, and attacks were prevented.

It was just past midnight—12:23 a.m., to be exact. I had just lain down on my bed, grateful for being able to retire at a reasonable hour for a change, when the sound of a screaming mortar round and then the explosion were heard right near our trailer. My trailer buddy and I immediately sat up in our beds, looking over at each other and anticipating additional rounds. Another one was heard that was way too close for comfort. But it was the silence afterward that was a little unsettling as we listened for additional explosions.

Then came the sound of helicopters, the customary sound of automatic weapon fire, and a few retaliatory explosions, signaling that the assailants were on the run. The CPA siren blasted, "Take cover! Take cover! This is not a test." We never doubted it was the real thing. We had been instructed to stay in our trailers and to take cover under the mattress of our beds, rather than running around trying to find more solid protection.

When the all-clear signal came, we returned to our beds, but my mind was still engaged in the emergencies of the day rather than the mortar explosions of the night. I had spent most of the week trying to keep my sources alive and out of jail. I had been building a file of information and evidence against several high-ranking officials in the Iraqi police department that I hoped would expose their trail of deceit and corruption. I was grouping our forces as I built my case against them, calling upon all the powers at hand to expedite their removal.

Greed had captured the hearts of so many, greed for money and power. We were continually fighting the battle of weeding out individuals who were trying to take advantage of the existing situation, with so much money floating around and so many new opportunities to snatch it. Each corrupt individual seemed to be like an octopus attaching a tentacle to anything within his reach, each one creating their own mini-network of corruption.

It was survival of the greediest, everyone grabbing as much as they could for themselves. There was no black and white, only a large gray area between what was thought to be right and wrong, with many people feeling like something was owed them for the years of suffering under Saddam's rule. There was a sense that everyone should take something while there was still something to take.

Sometimes the tables were turned so that the criminals went after the good guys with charges and accusations, putting them on the defensive with fabricated stories. It was difficult to know what the truth of the matter was, whose story to believe. With the counterfeiting gang, once they were released, they turned the charges back against our source, with the help of their crooked judge who issued a warrant for his arrest. They fabricated a story that he had broken into one of their homes and stolen several pieces of jewelry.

There was dishonesty, fraud, and corruption at the highest levels, touching every aspect of life there. The higher it went up through the government, the more difficult it was to terminate, with individual power bases growing and support widening. At times I ran up against people who had become so powerful that others in investigative organizations felt too small to tackle them. That was certainly the case with the top-ranking police officers at the police department; even Internal Affairs was afraid to go after them, fearing they or their families might be killed. It was difficult to see a solution in sight.

Sporadic explosions continued to remind us that we were still in Baghdad, still in a war zone. Even though things seemed to be getting better, with lulls in the action extending for several days, Iraq was still a nation plagued with evil. There were weeks when I spent most of my time simply trying to keep my sources alive and out of jail, due to the intricate web of corruption in high places. As I worked to build files of information and evidence against high-ranking officials, I could only hope that my efforts would aid in their exposure and, eventually, a real change for the better. Fortunately, our team of debriefers was unified in our desire to continue what we had started.

* * *

Fully supplied with a warehouse full of toys, I decided it was time for another sharing adventure. This time, my team and I traveled with Hazam, Azad, and my interpreter up north to a small city north of Arbil called Salahuddin, right in the middle of the Kurdish region. It was about four hours north of Baghdad. We went in two vehicles, Hazam's truck and Azad's Volvo. We filled Hazam's pickup truck with boxes of toys and took off.

We met with the mayor of the small town, who was expecting us. He had arranged for the neediest families in the village to gather the next morning with their children outside city hall to receive the goodies we had prepared for them. We were expecting about forty families to show up, but it turned out to be more like four hundred once word got out. They had entirely surrounded the building with children of all ages waiting for toys.

The Kurdish media was there to capture the moment. They certainly didn't expect to see this many people, all pressing forward, pushing up against the building. At one point, the kids began pounding on the windows of the city hall in hopes that we would pass toys through the windows. The Kurdish media later broadcast the episode to all the Kurdish satellite channels throughout the world.

Logistics became a problem as we tried to figure out how we were going to expedite the distribution of one toy to each child, ensuring that none made their way back in line to pick up another. Just getting all of them to line up in single file was a major undertaking. Getting them to then file through the door in an orderly fashion was easier said than done, with each child wanting to be at the front of the line for better selection.

All in all, it went really well, aside from the occasional outburst of anger from the adults inside the building, who were all attempting to tell us the best way to get the toys distributed. All of them seemed to have conflicting self-serving ideas, which in the end suited their own needs and desires for their children to have a toy. Despite the hassle, we gave out all of the toys we brought—and, fortunately, we had plenty of toys.

Once the word reached the clamoring people outside that all the toys had been distributed, a certain degree of calmness spread over the crowd. Using the toys that they had just received, the children began playing with each other. Catching the mood and spirit of the moment brought on by the children, we began playing a number of ring-around-the-rosy-type games. Holding their little hands, we ran around in circles, laughing and singing with them. Joy and happiness spread through the children, even affecting some of the adults as well.

The mayor was gracious to our team and grateful for our presence. He had taken us out to dinner the night before and again for pastries and coffee once the toys had been passed out. He invited us to come back, promising to make things a little more orderly the next time. Tragically, a few weeks later we received word that the mayor and his son were killed by a suicide bomber. My heart ached for them every time I recalled the joy and happiness we shared that day.

CHAPTER FOURTEEN

THE TYRANT IS A PRISONER

L adies and gentlemen, we got him," Ambassador Paul Bremer
announced. "The tyrant is a prisoner."

My cell phone lit up with one call after another as people near
and far called to share their excitement in hearing the news of
Saddam Hussein's capture. Iraqi friends and associates were calling
throughout the day to express their appreciation for what the United
States had done for them. Most Iraqis never imagined that such a day
would come in their lifetime.

Passengers on buses and trucks leaned out their windows and
shouted ecstatically: "They got him! They got Saddam!" Radio stations in Baghdad blared the news with celebratory music. Many resi-
dents fired small arms into the air in jubilation.

Iraqis could not believe the photos they saw in the morning
paper. It was Saddam Hussein—their former president, ruler, dictator, and almost deified leader. He was considered super-human,
magical and mystical, able to call upon the evil spirits from the other
side; he was Master of the Red Genie Tribe. There he was—dirty,
unshaven, with matted-down hair, crawling out of a rat hole—a
grey-bearded, homeless beggar.

"How could it be?" they asked out loud in amazement and disbelief. "How could it be like this?" Saddam, their strong and brave
leader, surrendered without a shot being fired, not even a shot to
end his own pathetic life. Where was the iron hand, the great military strategist, the courageous commander, the brutal murderer of
countless thousands?

121

PAUL HOLTON

Tracked down to his underground den, he was cornered like a rat. He was disheveled, powerless, and exhausted. He was suddenly demoted; he became a common man with no special powers that could whisk him away on a cloud of thunder or bring down lightning bolts upon his assailants.

The people of Iraq were rid of his tyranny forever. It was the end of the road for Saddam. He was now ready, as President Bush said, to "face the justice he denied to millions."

* * *

One day, as I was tooling around the Green Zone in the Chief Wiggles Toy Bus, I saw two little sisters, ages six and ten, walking into the zone through one of the gates. I had seen them selling candy in our parking lots on occasion, so I thought it would be a good idea to give them a ride.

They were both so cute and so serious about their work. Through my interpreter I learned that they went to school in the morning and sold their candy in the afternoon. Then these two little entrepreneurs let us in on their sales secret. They had a list of things to say in English, and they knew just how to pull on our heartstrings to get us to buy. The oldest would say in her sweetest voice, "I have no money," while tilting her head to the side and staring up at American soldiers with her big brown eyes. Like most, I am a total sucker for kids like that.

* * *

A team of CNN reporters was scheduled to travel with us on a trip to "Share Joys with Toys." I grabbed a quick bite to eat, knowing I would need the energy later on. I jumped in the bus for a quick jaunt over to the warehouse to load up the toys for the day's activities. We planned to go to an unfinished mosque, where about forty homeless families had settled in, and spend a couple of hours with the children.

With the bus half-full of toys, the team was ready in the parking lot—Hazam, Emad, Qies, my interpreter, the CNN crew, and Dr. Eaman, who was going to show us the way. I did the usual briefing as far as the order of vehicles and where we were going, and then off we went.

We made our way through the back streets of Baghdad, our four vehicles clinging to each other as if hooked together like cars of a train, making every effort not to allow another vehicle to slide in between our caravan. Even though it was hard to lose sight of a bus, we didn't want to take any chances. We had heard plenty of stories how the bad guys would try to break into convoys to single out a vehicle for attack.

The great thing about driving in Iraq was the absence of traffic laws—at least it seemed that way. Every driver had to fend for himself—it was total vehicular anarchy. Yet it was amazing how well the whole system worked with no traffic lights, no lanes, no rules or regulations, and no one to enforce them if there were any. Anything was legal out on the road; you could drive anywhere and any way you wanted. It was "survival of the biggest," so the bus fared quite well. As long as the nose of your vehicle was ahead of the cars around you, you were in charge. The front-seat passenger directed traffic from inside the car with synchronized hand gestures. Our loaded automatic weapons held tightly on our laps, just in case, gave fresh meaning to the term "riding shotgun."

It was a strange feeling to always have a 9mm pistol or an MP5 slung over one shoulder wherever I went, whether visiting a friend or buying ice cream or pizza. We had to always assume the worst was going to happen. Our motto was, "Locked and loaded, with a round in the chamber."

The unfinished Grand Mosque had become home to numerous families who had been evicted from their homes or apartments due to lack of money to pay for rent. Some families lived inside the unfinished structure, and many more lived in cinder-block shacks and shanties around the perimeter.

One man, the head of his neighborhood block, stepped forward to help organize the activity. He wrote down the name of each family so as not to forget anyone and to make for an orderly distribution of our bounty. We came loaded with a thousand dollars' worth of blankets and heaters, donated by the British owner of a clothing store, and of course, plenty of toys.

As we pulled up, a large crowd started to form, aware of our intentions and anticipating the free handouts. I exited my bus and quickly began shaking hands while offering the customary greetings of the morning. I made sure to extend my hand and offer up a smile to every man in the area. The women were all clustered together in their own group next to the men, in their long black *burkhas*, which covered all but their faces. Knowing their customs, I wasn't going to shake the women's hands, but not wanting to offend, I offered up a cheerful "Good morning." The children were cautiously hiding behind the legs of the adults, not sure what to think about the arrival of the Americans. But as expected, they warmed up to us right away.

Maintaining an orderly distribution to every family was often a challenge, so we instructed them all to return to their homes and wait for us to come to them. One by one, with all of us toting imported blankets and kerosene heaters, we visited each home, speaking with the father, the mother, and many of the children.

The families were extremely poor, evidenced by their ragged clothes, worn-out shoes, dirty appearance, and unsanitary living conditions. The kids were lacking in many things, most running around barefoot and with very little clothing on what was a chilly day. The flies seemed to be the only thing thriving in this area. The families lived in one-room mud huts without utilities such as electricity and running water.

As our team of givers went from house to house, several things about these families really impressed me. They were humble, gracious, and patient, and they were not ashamed of how they were living. They offered us tea, with several even asking us to stay for lunch. In contrast to all of the other toy drops, things went very orderly, with no one trying to get more than someone else.

After the parents received the blankets and heaters, we separated the kids into two groups, boys and girls. While the children were dancing round and round singing songs, I was in the middle, handing toys to each child. We gave out stuffed animals, toy cars, and many other things. The children were all well-behaved, with no pushing and shoving to get the best toys.

Between locations, we stopped for a bite of flatbread and hummus. The tasty flatbread that is served and eaten everywhere is baked in a cone-shaped earthen oven. It sits upright with a fire inside on the bottom and an opening on top. The vendor takes the shaped pieces of dough and slaps them hard against the walls of the brick oven where the bread cooks to perfection. I was amazed that the bread didn't fall off the sides of the oven into the fire.

From there we dashed off to a children's hospital to visit the oncology ward where the leukemia patients were. We had just enough toys and stuffed animals for each child to get a couple of items. I was so pleased that we could offer up a small token of love to those overlooked and suffering children.

It was difficult to witness what these children were going through. We were deeply affected by the courage of both the mothers and the children, and we stopped by each bed to chat with them where possible. It was painful to realize that many of these children would not live to see their next birthday. The toys made a real difference, bringing a smile to the youngest and most innocent victims of Saddam's horrifying regime.

Children in the Oncology ward are happy to receive toys and stuffed animals.

* * *

My time in Iraq was rapidly coming to a close. With only two months left before I returned home, my pace quickened and my focus sharpened. I endeavored to finish everything I had started. I felt a sense of urgency, knowing my time was getting short and I had much left to accomplish. With only so much time in a day, I was trying to get more organized and directed, my daily to-do lists growing longer and longer. I had stopped exercising and doing any other expendable activity in order to finish all the projects I had started. Sleep had even taken a backseat to work.

Unexpectedly, I was hit by the news that my father, who was then eighty-four, had just been diagnosed with colon cancer, the doctor giving him only a few months to live. He had been remarkably healthy all of his life, but he was now unable to eat and required intravenous feeding. He had been hospitalized for the past few days and was being moved to a care center where he was told he would spend the remaining days of his life.

A wiry, dark-haired, and spunky kid, my dad grew up on a cattle ranch in Colorado and learned the value of hard physical labor before he started school. When Pearl Harbor was attacked, he showed his commitment to God, country, and hard work by enlisting in the Air Force, where he distinguished himself in the Pacific Theater. On Okinawa, at the height of the conflict there, it was discovered that he was color-blind, something that should have been found before he ever left the ground. As a result, he was delayed from flying with his normal flight team that day. Miraculously for him, he was not on the plane when it was shot down by the enemy and all aboard were killed. A deeply religious man, he saw that as a sign that he still had important work God wanted him to do. I guess one of those tasks was to raise a son named Paul. The impact of his example and teachings can be seen in everything I do, both the silly and the significant. I hoped the Lord would grant him one more miracle and allow me to get home in time.

* * *

Our earlier visit to the homeless families living around the mosque was prompted by Omar, a young boy who was concerned with the plight of the homeless children at his school. He told his mother of the need, and she relayed the request to us. In recognition of his concern and efforts, we went to his school to make a presentation.

We pulled up to the school with a team of ambassadors of joy, toys in hand. It was strange, but understandable, to see several armed guards out in front of the elementary school. There had been several bomb threats at schools by individuals trying to disrupt and destabilize the situation. On one occasion, due to our intelligence, a bomb in a backpack at a school was discovered, removed, and diffused. The thought of a bomb going off in a crowded schoolyard made me shudder.

Stopping at the school office, we spent a few minutes speaking with the principal about the purpose for our visit. This middle-aged Iraqi woman, educated and devoted to her school children, was thrilled by our desire to recognize her student. I was impressed by her desire to offer an education for the homeless children when other schools had turned them away.

With the principal leading the way, our team went to Omar's classroom. It was a great moment for him as we presented a letter of appreciation from the CPA and several nice gifts made possible by donations from home. We gave him an artist's kit with a full array of pencils, paints, markers, and a built-in easel. It was specially selected for Omar, a promising young artist.

As he stood in front of his class to receive the award, he just beamed, so eager to show his class what he had received. We took a class photo and encouraged the others to follow his example.

* * *

Many of my sources refused to be seen at the CPA palace for fear of being recognized by one of the Iraqi employees. As a result, I had been conducting more of my business at lunch and dinner meetings, both in and outside the Green Zone. There was one small corner cafe within the Green Zone that was particularly conducive to those meetings, serving up a tasty sampling of local cuisine and Iraqinized American food.

Since I was spending a good part of my day in this Green Zone cafe, the owner of the establishment assigned me a permanent parking space, with a hand-written sign that said, "Reserved for Chief Wiggles." I got to know all the employees quite well, often popping back into the kitchen to dance with the kitchen help to a song playing over the speakers. Everyone clapped while singing along to a popular Arabic tune with me. Spontaneous moments like those only increased my love for these people.

One evening after my meetings at the cafe, I was sitting outside our hooch, waiting for my ride to pick me up. A car drove into our area with several Iraqis inside. As they pulled around to the front door, one of our interpreters dashed out to jump into their car, obviously being picked up to go somewhere. This was not a big deal, but I was alarmed by who I saw driving the car. The driver was the right-hand man of Chief Ahmed of the police department, who we had been actively investigating since the counterfeiting bust.

Because of the nature of my business, I had enemies out there that would definitely take action against me if they could. If my enemies knew where I lived, once inside the Green Zone, they could really mess with me; I would be in serious jeopardy. This represented a major breech of security and potentially compromised my mission. From that day forward, I had clear reasons to be even more concerned about my safety.

* * *

My alarm went off at 5:00 a.m. on Christmas morning, indicating it was time for another one of our "Sharing Joys with Toys" excursions. Our two-day Christmas vacation allowed us the additional time we needed to take our toys to some previously untouched areas, including some areas up north.

We had the truck about half full when the mortars started coming in from just outside the Green Zone. I didn't hear any of them hit nearby, but I felt it might be a good idea to take cover. All of us dashed into the basement of the adjoining building. With its tin roof and tin walls, our warehouse, even though guarded by tanks, would have been no match for any incoming projectiles.

We waited until the explosions stopped, which ended up being about an hour or so, before venturing back out. There was a lot of return fire from what sounded like Apache helicopters. Automatic weapon bursts were heard around the area, indicating that the insurgent thugs were on the run.

With the truck packed high with toys and clothes, we made a quick stop to meet up with Azad in another vehicle full of volunteers anxious to participate in our toy delivery. We always traveled with at least two vehicles for safety and security reasons. With at least two fully loaded automatic weapons per vehicle, we departed. There was an unmistakable paradox as we departed to deliver toys to children, all equipped with AK-47s, MP5s, and various other weapons. I was personally armed with a pistol and an MP5 for my protection. If you hadn't seen the toys, you might have thought we were going out on a raid.

We traveled for several hours, making our way up north into Kurdish territory near the border of Turkey. Once we arrived in the town of Duhok, we picked up an Iraqi pediatrician who was anxious to guide us to our destination. In addition to his pediatric practice, he focused special attention on the psychological issues of children being raised in such difficult circumstances.

Leaving the paved highway, we made our way up a dirt road past a large open market. We pulled up to what appeared to be an old prison on top of a small hill. As if entering a large castle, we drove through an opening into the spacious, open courtyard in the center of the building.

The doctor referred to this as "the compound" and began to describe the history of the building. It had been used as a prison back in the late 1990s to incarcerate, torture, and kill hundreds of Kurdish people at the hands of Saddam's special military unit. As I glanced around, I could see that the courtyard was encircled by hundreds of small rooms, with no facilities or amenities—just dark gray walls surrounded by dirt.

The rooms were occupied by otherwise homeless people, many of whom had lost a loved one at this facility, which explained why so many of the women were without husbands. There were over two hundred families with some eight hundred children living at this site of imprisonment, torture, and death.

At first glance I couldn't see many children, but no sooner had we entered the compound than children began to run out from every door and alley. Within minutes, we were surrounded by squealing and laughing children as they began to figure out the purpose of our visit.

After meeting with the compound mayor, we decided to have all the children return to their homes so we could visit with them one by one. It sounded like a good idea, but in actuality the children were too excited to stay inside and patiently await our arrival at their doorstep. Even so, we enforced the instruction by telling them to all return to their homes.

With a small group of men carrying our boxes, we proceeded to the first room in one corner of the building. Over the next five hours, we went from room to room, handing out toys to every family. There were families in every nook and cranny, holed up in every corridor and usable area. There were even families on the roof of the building in makeshift homes, built out of sheets of wood, paneling, or metal.

Conditions for those people were sparse. There were shared bathrooms and shared kitchens in some areas, while others had built in a gas stove to have their own kitchen. Most were without doors, and the opening to each home was covered with a blanket or a tarp. Old worn-out blankets or pieces of carpeting covered the cold cement floors of the homes.

I quickly visited with the mothers of those beautiful children who had surrounded us in the courtyard. There were no toys to be seen in any of the homes—no dolls, no toy trucks, no stuffed animals. The rooms were bare—only a few homes had furniture, a

Christmas Day in the Dahukin hospital

television, or any appliances. There were no closets or bedrooms, just one room for the entire family, and in some cases there were as many as ten people living in one room.

The mothers would line their children up in their simply appointed homes as I handed a carefully selected toy to each one. The children were so delighted to receive such an unexpected gift that they would jump up and down while holding it tightly to their chest. Their eyes lit up, and happiness filled the room.

As we entered some homes, the mothers could be seen putting on their young daughters' finest little dresses as they prepared for our arrival. They really wanted to make a good impression on us; they greeted us with dignity, not embarrassment.

Children crowded in behind us as we walked from one home to the next. Some kids, hoping to get another toy, would sneak in line with the kids from another family; but I was too quick at catching them in their act of deception. It was all done in good fun and laughter.

There were several little girls who would fight through the crowd of kids to hold my hand while I walked along, each time grabbing my hand again after exiting a home. They grabbed onto my clothes and my legs as I moved around the complex.

On many occasions the families begged me to stay for lunch or tea, hoping I would linger. But with so many families and so many children, we moved along as fast as we could, hoping to finish before it started to rain. I was overcome at times with emotion, as I quickly visited with the mothers of those beautiful children. I cannot begin to put into words how I felt as I witnessed such poverty on the one hand and such joy from the children on the other. But the rain came, bringing an end to a marvelous day full of both happiness and sorrow. Tired and wet, we left the compound well rewarded.

* * *

Back in my CPA palace office, sitting behind the Mother of All Desks, it was easy to become somewhat insulated from the gruesome realities of war. Hearing the concussion of an exploding bomb is not the same as seeing someone bleeding from a bomb blast. Seeing the strafing on a building from rapid arms fire is not the same as tending to those wounded by gunfire. Reading a body count report is not the same thing as seeing a dead body. I knew that my insulation left me with a somewhat distorted view of the war. Never once did I fire my weapon, but every time I pulled it to my shoulder, I knew I could be responsible for ending someone's life.

Our trip to Duhok shoved the reality of death right into my line of sight. As I was driving along the highway leading back to Baghdad, I looked to the side of the road and saw a dead Iraqi man lying in the ditch. His body was twisted and sprawled as if he had just been tossed out the door of a moving car. He was bloated and swollen beyond description. The smell stung my eyes and my throat. I gasped for air as I felt waves of nausea hit me like a Mack truck.

I suspect that this unknown man was a victim of Iraq's internal struggle. This poor fellow was probably involved in the black market—a readily available income source for Iraqis—and made a poor decision that had riled organized crime leaders. But it was still unsettling to come face-to-face with such an irreverent and brutal death.

Death is the vicious unseen partner in every war strategy. It reminded me of why we wanted this struggle settled once and for all.

CHAPTER FIFTEEN

TO VICTORY

C hief, you've got forty-eight hours to remove yourself from the CPA."

That was all the notice I received that my mission was over. The phone call came from a colonel working under General Fast. The colonel told me to pack up my stuff and move myself to Camp Victory, not far from Baghdad International Airport (BIAP). He instructed me not to talk to anyone. I was to have no contact with anyone outside of my immediate team members.

I asked him what this was all about. It was abrupt. It was mysterious. It was unnerving. I tried to get any bit of information about why this was happening and why I couldn't have more time. He made it clear that he had called to give orders, not answers. I was assured someone at Camp Victory would be talking to me.

I was in shock after such an unexpected phone call. I didn't know where to begin. I didn't know how to end. Thoughts of all my unfinished work whirred through my head as I tried to pull myself together. After making several attempts to delay my sudden departure, I complied with my orders to leave the palace.

The next two days passed like a desert sandstorm, propelling me into a whole new experience—one for which I was unprepared. I was deeply saddened to be hastily separated from the people I had grown to love: my fellow teammates, my interpreters, my colleagues at the CPA, and my dear Iraqi friends. As I made my rounds throughout the CPA and the Green Zone to say good-bye, there were many tender moments as I bid farewell to people I suspected I would never see again.

I had a hard time imagining life without my teammates. What would I do without them? What would they do without me? They were my lifeblood, my best friends. As I considered my unfinished work, I was grateful to know there was someone in the office who could continue working on the case against Chief Ahmed of the police department.

What about the work of Operation Give? Who was going to keep the work going? How were the toys going to get delivered?

It was extremely hard to part with the two captains, Qies and Emad, who had become such an integral part of our Operation Give team; Dr. Eaman, to whom I'd grown so close; and my interpreter, who had been with me every step of the way.

* * *

Chief Allen, along with two other teammates, Baghdaddy and Sergeant Charm, accompanied me to Camp Victory as a way to show their moral support for my predicament. With all of us loaded into the patrol vehicle, we drove away from the CPA palace, saying good-bye to my life in the heart of the new Iraq. As we drove away, I waved good-bye to my faithful Iraqi friends, Qies and Emad, who were waiting in the parking lot. With tears in my eyes, I said a final farewell to my interpreter. It was a quiet drive from the CPA over to Camp Victory, a one-vehicle cortege. I had many thoughts racing through my head, all lapsing into uncertainty.

Camp Victory was on the southwest side of Baghdad, closer to the airport and inside the grounds of one of Saddam's other palaces. My teammates unloaded my gear at one of the tents so I could get settled in. As I watched my comrades drive off, there was a knot of unknowns twisting in my stomach. I had been kicked out of the kingdom, ostracized from the CPA palace that had been my home for the past six months, and dropped off without a word of instruction about what was going to happen. I was only told to report to the main office the next day.

In the morning, I reported to the officer in charge of me. She just told me that someone would be in touch with me. Every day, for the next three weeks, I would walk up the dirt road from my tent to the main office. Each morning I asked the officer for an update on my situation. Each morning I began my long hours of waiting for someone who was supposed to talk to me. No one had an answer for me. The uncertainty was killing me.

Everyone else just went about their work as if I wasn't there. I had become a non-entity. With only a month remaining on my tour of duty, I found downtime frustrating. So little to do and so frustrated for the little time that was left. It was as if aliens had snatched me up from my hectic, purposeful, and meaningful existence at the CPA, only to drop me off on an island full of people who were unable to see me or hear me.

Many acquaintances, former friends, and superior officers treated me as if I had leprosy, refusing at times to even acknowledge my presence when passing by. Preposterous rumors spread through the camp as others questioned my purgatorial existence, falsely suspecting me of selling illegal weapons and other such ludicrous explanations. All this time not a word was heard from any of those who were at one time my direct chain of command.

I spent my time over the next three weeks just sitting. There were no duties, no assignments, and no responsibilities. I looked forward to mealtime just to break up the monotony. The daily question-and-answer session was the same. "Is there someone here who can meet with me?"

"Not today."

I was alone except for my CPA team, who would show up every few days to check on my condition. Fortunately, there were also two captains from my home unit working at the same facility, who took me under their wing during this difficult time. But it was the unknown that was eating me alive—the stress of not knowing what this all meant.

The rest of my tent-mates didn't return until around 10:30 p.m., when their shift ended. It seemed odd to be in such quiet surroundings after having spent the last six months working late every night at the CPA palace with several of my close friends. I missed the rigor of the CPA, where people were still actively pursuing their daily activities late into the night.

The winter air was cold, forming puffs of vapor as I spoke. I felt unprepared for the briskness of the evening with my cold-weather gear packed away in one of my three duffle bags. At night, not wanting to pull out my sleeping bag, I wrapped myself in a blanket and poncho liner. I resumed an acquaintance with my trusty old cot, after believing I had graduated from that lifestyle.

Occasional explosions broke up the silence of the evening as I sat alone at the far end of a tent, which was my new home. Within seconds, the sound of sirens blaring could be heard in the distance. A few minutes later, jets could be heard overhead, further securing the safety of our surroundings. The unmistakable sounds of war did nothing to diminish my heightened state of anxiety.

During this time of personal difficulty, there was a glimmer of peace about me as I felt God letting me know that everything was going to work out and that this series of unwelcome events was all part of a larger plan. I spent much of my time reading, pondering, and reconnecting with my spiritual self, tapping into the heavenly powers that had accompanied me during other challenging times in my life.

* * *

Finally, I heard through my teammates that an investigative officer had been assigned to my case and had questioned them about my conduct, my letter-writing activities, and my involvement with the toy drive. Apparently, the letter I had written about Chief Ahmed of the police department upset a few people back in Washington. In my letter, I made no specific accusations about the Chief, but I did suggest that his record and behavior deserved further scrutiny.

Finally, some information about my case started emerging. I learned I would be staying at Camp Victory for as long as it took for the military to finish the investigation, then off for a short stay in Kuwait as a stepping-stone on my journey home.

February 7, 2004, marked my one-year anniversary of being gone from home, mobilized for Operation Iraqi Freedom. My days were now slowing down to a virtual standstill. As I continued to wait for the outcome of the investigation, new replacements arrived from the States, and the majority of my group prepared for their journey home. It was distressing to watch these comings and goings as I languished in military limbo. The Army had given me no indication whether or not I would be joining my group for the return trip home. I was stranded in some kind of suspended animation until such time as they decided what to do with me. Strangely, I was at peace, even while living in an area where background noises consisted of frequent bursts of automatic weapon fire and loud explosions.

Except for the bare essentials, my gear was packed and ready to go as I entered the last phase of my deployment. If all went well with the investigation, I expected to return home with the rest of my original National Guard unit, but that was yet to be determined.

My pals from the CPA continued to come by every few days to update me on what they had heard about my case. Most of the time they didn't have much new information, but I appreciated their short visits and continual words of encouragement. Each of them gave me their take on what was going on after they were questioned by the investigative officer. They informed me on the line of questioning, which revealed for the first time why I was being investigated.

It appeared that the military was concerned about both the letter I wrote to the Governing Council and my work with Operation Give. My buddies told me they had just learned it was against Army regulations for a serviceman to solicit donations. I swallowed hard as we said our good-byes.

After they left, I was alone—really alone—and the isolation was taking its toll. As I pondered my uncertain situation, it suddenly occurred to me that I might be in deeper trouble than I had thought. What I had previously assumed was just a minor infraction had become something much more serious. Had my desire to bless Iraqi children tarnished my military service? Had my insistence on investigating corruption jeopardized my future? Had I put my family at risk? Was the full weight of the military justice system going to come crashing down on my head? My heart was pounding, my palms were sweating, and sleep was impossible. This was more stressful than incoming Scuds on the first night of the war.

To some degree, the wait was over. After interviewing all those associated or acquainted with me in any way, the investigative officer, Lieutenant Colonel Jones, finally made his way to Camp Victory to lay things out for me. Now into my third week of waiting, I was able to question him about what was going on. He was appalled to learn that I had been waiting so long without contact from anyone in my chain of command. He agreed that it was troubling that so many military comrades had distanced themselves from me like rats leaving a sinking ship. He was also bothered by the fact that no one had told me what the issues were.

Lieutenant Colonel Jones was preparing to return home upon completion of this investigative assignment. Thankfully, we both had the same goal—finish the investigation and leave Iraq as soon as possible. He was kind enough to lay out the plan for the next couple of weeks, schedule a time to question me, and inform me what the procedure would be. He seemed highly professional, someone who would handle my case with fairness and integrity.

Lieutenant Colonel Jones' questioning lasted several days and covered every imaginable aspect of my work, contacts, and activities. He didn't badger me, but he was excruciatingly thorough. He was clearly after something. I was nervous, afraid, uncertain of the outcome, and unsure of the ramifications. The tables had turned. The interrogator was being interrogated. My days were filled with plenty of things to pray about.

It was apparent from his line of questioning that the military was uneasy about the time I spent on Operation Give. Was it interfering with my work? Whose vehicle was I using to make these toy drops? Whose computer was I using? It seemed that they were searching for anything they could use against me. I was beginning to feel that I had crossed some invisible line.

I was summoned to a meeting to review what had been determined in my case up to this point. I was seated on a chair across the room, while Lieutenant Colonel Jones was going over his findings with the Judge Advocate General (JAG) attorneys. They were just far enough away that I couldn't make out what they were saying. Periodically, Lieutenant Colonel Jones would approach me for a clarification and then rejoin the JAGs. They finally reached a stage where I could be included. The discussion was formal, somber, and rather threatening. Their faces made it clear that things were looking pretty bleak. They walked me through various scenarios, none of them pleasant. This appeared to be the beginning of a fairly lengthy process, and no one seemed optimistic about the outcome.

Suddenly, a messenger entered the room to relay a message. Once granted permission to speak, he said, "I have a message for Chief Paul Holton." I was already in hot water; I couldn't help but wonder how much deeper it was about to get.

The attorneys pointed to me. The messenger turned and proceeded to tell me, "Call your commander back in Salt Lake City at once. President Bush is trying to get in touch with you. The President wants to have breakfast with you at the White House." I'm sure that everyone heard me almost choke.

"Stop everything," the JAG attorney said as he closed the file and stowed his legal briefs.

The tone of the meeting and the direction of the investigation had just been turned on its head. If the Commander-in-Chief was going to recognize my efforts with Operation Give, military attorneys weren't about to stand in the way.

I called home at once, and after speaking with both my commander and my wife, I was instructed to call President Bush's senior speechwriter on the White House staff immediately. The message originally delivered wasn't completely accurate. The President actually just wanted to applaud my efforts in getting toys to Iraqi children and needed my permission to quote from my blog and discuss what I was doing.

I phoned the White House immediately to inquire about the nature of their interest. "The President is giving a speech during the annual National Prayer Breakfast on Thursday and would like to discuss certain details about Chief Wiggles and the toys," the President's speechwriter advised me.

"Of course, that would be great," I responded. I felt honored to receive that kind of recognition from my Commander-in-Chief. Frankly, I was surprised that knowledge of Operation Give had reached the White House.

With the speechwriter on the phone, I confirmed details about the success of Operation Give and granted permission to use a quote from my Chief Wiggles blog.

As I walked back along the dirt road toward my tent, I rejoiced at the miraculous event that had just taken place. I found a secluded area, free from others walking by, and knelt in prayer. As I considered this miracle, I found myself overcome with gratitude. Tears streamed down my cheeks as I tried to grasp the meaning of it all. The President of the United States was going to applaud my efforts with Operation Give.

Lieutenant Colonel Jones submitted his report to his superior officers with the President's remarks positioned on the top of his findings. He was confident that the presidential commendation would turn the tide for me and would ultimately result in a favorable outcome. What a turnaround. I felt as though I could have flown home without a jet.

* * *

With almost all of my tent-mates packed up and on their way to Kuwait and the tents at Camp Victory virtually empty, I was transferred to the military base at BIAP. It was like any other US military base, with almost no evidence I was still in Iraq.

It was great seeing Major Price for the first time in six months. We embraced in a big, manly bear hug as we saw each other again. There were only three of us from our unit left in Iraq—Major Price, Captain Hult, and me. The rest of the group had already made its way to Camp Doha near Kuwait City and was waiting for us to join them. We would be at Camp Doha for a couple of weeks, then off to Fort Carson for a week or so, and, if all went well, back on home turf by the first part of March.

The two officers had each decided to stick around until I was given the green light to leave, even though they were both chomping at the bit to get out of town. It was reassuring to know I had friends who would stick by me when needed. But, with no end in sight to the waiting game, they were each beginning to wonder if, at some point, they would have to leave without me.

At BIAP, the showers were hot and the porta-potties were clean. Add to this a fully equipped morale, welfare, and recreation (MWR) room with loads of movies, and it made this holding pen almost enjoyable. To top it off, Major Price and I had a room with a heater and a vehicle to share.

Then came the unexpected news that finally got me on my way. My wife called to inform me that my father's colon cancer was in its final stages, with doctors giving him only weeks to live. Not knowing how long the Army was going to take to make a final decision, I told my wife to arrange a Red Cross message calling me home. After much diligence on her part, she finally got someone at the Red Cross to issue the request.

The Red Cross message arrived, requesting the Army release me to care for my dying father. Within a few hours the arrangements were made for me to return to the States for an undetermined period of time. Now the three of us were finally able to link up with the rest of our men down at Camp Doha.

In anticipation of things to come, I awakened at 4:30 a.m., Friday the 13th. In the crisp morning air, with a Humvee and a trailer loaded down with all our bags, we departed for the airport.

After sitting in the waiting room with hundreds of other homebound soldiers, our flight was finally called up for its departure at 11:30 a.m. We loaded up the C-130, sat inside its barren hull, facing each other in our webbed seats, for a quick hour-and-a-half flight down to Kuwait City. I was finally out of Iraq.

After unloading from the plane, I sat in the parking lot of the airport, watching over our gear. I experienced a flashback of the thoughts and feelings I had a year ago when I arrived at that same airfield. For a moment, when I felt the sand-filled wind against my face and the noise of tents flapping in the wind, I thought it was beginning all over again.

I was snapped back to reality by hearing Major Price's voice. "How'd ya like a foot-long Subway sandwich?" Just knowing there was now a Subway franchise on base was all I needed to let me know that I had taken a giant step closer to home.

I was leaving, not arriving.

CHAPTER SIXTEEN

BACK TO THE BEGINNING

As I walked into the bay of our group's living quarters at Camp Doha, each of the men in my home unit greeted me warmly. Outside of just a few individuals, I had not seen any of them since leaving Camp Bucca some six months earlier, and for many it had been the entire year.

We had all been greatly blessed, and by the grace of God, we all made it back healthy and alive—not even a serious injury. It was a great reunion, filled with renewed love for each other. It was a group of men like no other.

One year earlier, we were thrown to the winds, scattered all over Iraq. As I walked through the bay past their bunks, I greeted them, embraced them, high-fived them, or patted them on the back. I was anxious to hear about their various escapades. Each had a remarkable story of great things they had accomplished.

Because of my dad's condition, I was only able to spend a couple of days at Camp Doha. I was taking an early emergency leave home to check on his condition, not wanting to experience another death in my immediate family in my absence. I stayed just long enough to out-process, making sure to turn in all the required equipment and take all of the necessary briefings, so that if at all possible, I wouldn't have to come back.

I am proud that I had the opportunity to serve my country in Iraq and to have participated in a great historical event—the toppling of Saddam Hussein. I'm grateful I was able to serve the cause of freedom and to build and uplift the Iraqi people. I will always be grateful for my family, who understood and sustained my desire to fulfill this mission.

* * *

What began as a simple gesture, sharing a toy with a child in Iraq, has grown to touch the lives of millions. President Bush recognized this effort in his remarks at the 52nd Annual National Prayer Breakfast in Washington, DC, on February 5, 2004:

> "Our people in uniform understand the high calling they have answered because they see the nation and the lives they are changing. A guardsman from Utah named Paul Holton has described seeing an Iraqi girl crying and decided then and there to help that child and others like her. By enlisting aid through the Internet, Chief Warrant Officer Holton had arranged the shipment of more than 1,600 aid packages from overseas. Here's how this man defines his own mission: 'It is part of our heritage that the benefits of being free, enjoyed by all Americans, were set up by God, intended for all people. Bondage is not of God, and it is not right that any man should be in bondage at any time, in any way.' Everyone in this room can say amen to that.
>
> "There's another part of our heritage we are showing in Iraq, and that is the great American tradition of religious tolerance. The Iraqi people are mostly Muslims, and we respect the faith they practice. Our troops in Iraq have helped to refurbish mosques, have treated Muslim clerics with deference, and are mindful of Islam's holy days. Some of our troops are Muslims themselves, because America welcomes people of every faith. Christians and Jews and Muslims have too often been divided by old suspicions, but we are called to act as what we are—the sons and daughters of Abraham.
>
> "Our work in a troubled part of the world goes on, and what we have begun, we will finish. In the years of challenge, our country will remain strong, and strong of heart. And as we meet whatever test might come, let us never be too proud to acknowledge our dependence on Providence and to take our cares to God."

The President's remarks and other reports fueled a groundswell of public support for Operation Give. This outpouring of donations has enabled Operation Give to grow and expand its work, not only to the children of Iraq but also to others facing critical needs such as the victims of the December 2004 tsunami in Southeast Asia. The need is great. The work goes on. And the generosity of the American people is boundless.

* * *

From my point of view, it seemed that our involvement did not hinge on whether or not we uncovered Saddam's buried WMDs. Finding WMDs wasn't the focus of Operation Iraqi Freedom. Our success or failure in Operation Iraqi Freedom, as the name suggests, was about securing freedom for the Iraqi people. That's what we were really fighting for. Freedom for that oppressed nation hopefully would lead to stabilizing a volatile and dangerous region of the world.

I remain convinced that this was about the Iraqi people, more specifically the children, the next generation of Iraqis. This was a chance for them to be free from the controlling grasp of Saddam Hussein. We had given the Iraqis high hopes in times past as we appeared to come to their rescue, only to pull away when international opinion forced us to abandon our plans. We stood by while Saddam murdered thousands of Iraqi and Kurdish people who had risen up, showing their defiance, only to be squashed by this brutal tyrant.

I am not ashamed to say that, to a certain extent, it was also about oil. In this case, the lifeblood of the world economy was being held hostage by a self-serving, ruthless dictator who continued to squander the nation's riches to suit his brutal penchant for murder, torture, and regional aggression. Our action was about bringing security, peace, and prosperity to a people and to an important part of the world. We saw the potential of bringing jobs, income, and opportunities to the masses of the world family in the Middle East.

But these reasons do not fully explain what propelled me into the life-changing experiences I encountered serving in Iraq. I was motivated by a higher force—one that enlightened my mind and enhanced my abilities. I witnessed divine intervention on numerous occasions, bringing about a sequence of interconnected events that could not have happened by chance. I saw results achieved in miraculous ways, ruling out the possibility of intervention by any other power or force. Hurdles were overcome, obstacles were removed, paths were cleared, and, more than anything else, people were changed by the hand of God. Children's perspectives and attitudes about the US military and about the future were perhaps changed with every generous offering of kindness. Perhaps they will grow up telling their children about how the Americans came to their town, their home, their school and gave them a toy or a stuffed animal. Perhaps there will be collateral kindness spreading from generation to generation.

The overwhelming majority of the soldiers I worked with carried this mission in their hearts and performed this mission with unrelenting energy throughout their tours of duty. We knew we could free Iraqis from the chains of bondage, but we also needed to show them what to do with this freedom as responsible citizens. Our lives exemplified the benefits and the responsibilities of a democratic society.

By spending time in the homes of Iraqis, I experienced their culture, tasted their hospitality, and saw through their eyes. My glimpse into their souls revealed their fears, concerns, weaknesses, and desires for their children's future. They openly expressed their love for us as fellow brothers and sisters, with hope for a brighter future for Iraq without the crushing despotism of Saddam Hussein.

All of us at Hazim's house

My path was always prepared before me, as an intertwined sequence of events preceded my arrival at any given station. The hand of the Almighty touched individuals' hearts, softened their souls, and opened their eyes, to the end that many things moved smoothly along to resolution, in a totally unexpected manner. Miracle after miracle occurred as I traveled around that country.

The success of this operation was not in any of our hands; we were only tools in the Master's hands to bring about His desired results. It was not our vision, but His, that we were pursuing.

There was much outside of our line of sight as we moved forward into unknown areas. We knew we were imperfect but that our successes would outweigh our mistakes. Our desire was that, as common men and women, we could perform uncommon feats to bring about the long-term development of these people and this new nation.

There is a human face on the war in Iraq, and I saw it every day. The humanity, warmth, and love of the Iraqi people were made evident to me time and time again. The light was turned on again in the eyes of the Iraqi children, a light of hope and possibilities.

While in Iraq, I found myself as I discovered a passion for helping the people of Iraq, who had been without freedom or opportunity for decades. The work is far from complete. I still have higher aspirations to do something of greater value and to make a difference in any way I can.

We, as Americans and members of the human family, cannot sit idly by while we watch a society being overrun by men driven by selfish aspirations for power, wealth, and control. We must choose to take some initiative in stopping these forces, so that the children of the world have hope for a brighter tomorrow. We cannot ignore the problems of the day, assuming they will disappear before our children will have to deal with them. The children of the world are our future. The future lies in what they can see, but we must paint a picture of hope. Many active duty military have painted that picture with their own sweat and blood.

CHAPTER SEVENTEEN

THE NEED IS GREAT

After a steady stream of life-changing events in Iraq, I felt compelled, upon my return, to continue the work I had started with Operation Give. An outpouring of generosity from the American people had enabled our organization to grow, evolve, and achieve phenomenal results.

I was encouraged by the interest that some news media had in Chief Wiggles and Operation Give. Once they understood what we were trying to do, they were anxious to catch a quick interview with me and hear our story. Even more exciting was the outpouring of generosity from family, friends, and neighbors back home who wanted to contribute to "Share Joys with Toys." This kindness grew and expanded beyond just family and friends as thousands of Americans previously unknown to me contributed their time and resources to the work of Operation Give.

With a new determination and conviction to continue on the path I had begun, I returned to the States to resume my normal life as a Worldwide Account Manager with FedEx. Of course I had missed my wife and children tremendously over the past year and longed to spend as much time with them as possible, hoping to make up for all the lost time. My wife had done a great job of managing things in my absence but was ready to hand over the reigns to me again.

You see, without her support, I could have done nothing. The best part about it was that my loving wife had also succumbed to my contagious spirit and had begun in her own way to gather up toys and supplies. Early on she had been very instrumental in sending over all of my individual special request items. She had caught the fever of the work and did everything she could to help and support the cause.

The work proved to be more contagious than anyone imagined, and it quickly spread to many others who came forward volunteering to help. Not long after my return, I received a call from Elaine Ward, an incredible women who wanted to get involved in any way she could. Early on, Elaine put in countless hours to assist in perpetuating the mission of Operation Give. Even after a long struggle with bone cancer and the eventual amputation of one of her legs, she was unstoppable. With her tenacity and dedication, she fearlessly assisted in making it all come together.

Having been so abruptly yanked from my position at the CPA in the Green Zone, I had no choice but to turn over everything to the only person in Iraq that I trusted, Dr. Eaman. Having proven herself on numerous occasions, I knew that her heart was in the right place and she would ensure the right thing was done. With her as the lead and the two captains as her assistants, my heart and mind were at peace, because I knew that if anyone would be able to continue what I had started in Iraq, she would. Operation Give was in good hands.

Stacks of donations in our warehouse

With my absence and subsequent return to the States, I lost the warehouse space in the Green Zone and the ability to ship items through the military APO system. But even before I left Iraq, Dr. Eaman found a place to put all of the boxes of donated items. At her own expense, she paid for a new warehouse location outside the protection of the US military and managed the distribution of all the donations we had collected. The operation hardly skipped a beat.

Dr. Eaman was not afraid to stand up for what was right. Bravely, she stood her ground against Iraqi men in high positions in the government (which is unheard of in the Middle Eastern culture) if she felt they were exhibiting the wrong attitude or behavior. She worked tirelessly at her own expense and at the risk of losing her life to perpetuate the work of providing for suffering Iraqi children. She was targeted by insurgents on numerous occasions, even attacked at gunpoint. One time, three assailants, who attempted to kill her, attacked her in her car, only to be fought off as they watched her speed away.

With the loss of my military-aided logistical operations came a whole new solution, which seemed to miraculously fall into place upon my return. FedEx was the first to step up to the plate with an offer to ship several (actually it was more like ten) forty-foot ocean containers and an annual budget of free shipping for domestic shipments. This enabled people anywhere in the US to ship donated items to me in Salt Lake City, Utah, for free and allowed us in turn to ship container loads to the Civil Military Operations Center (CMOC) in Kuwait City, Kuwait. Working closely with the CMOC, we arranged for the contents of the containers to be moved by the military to Dr. Eaman's non-profit organization, set up as part of Operation Give.

FedEx offered to handle Operation Give's shipping needs

My best friend from high school, Gordon Hanks, was the next to volunteer a much-needed part to our eventual solution. He was the president of Bridgepoint Systems, a large distributor of carpet cleaning supplies and equipment. He offered to provide us with warehouse space for the constant flow of incoming donated items delivered by FedEx. Before I knew it, twenty or thirty pallets were stacked six feet high on the second floor of his warehouse. He was a real godsend and a key part of our ability to move forward.

Operation Give had significant assistance in the early stages from such companies as Clorox, Forever Young International, JibJab, and other corporate sponsors, who graciously provided us with resources in the form of monetary contributions, product donations, and promotional consideration. But the bedrock of support for Operation Give was the thousands of individual donors and volunteers. It was amazing to watch Americans everywhere spearhead their own grassroots donation drives in church groups, Boy Scout troops, schools, and neighborhoods. Many more simply visited us at www.operation-give.org to make a monetary donation. Even though the lifeblood of our organization was made up of volunteers, contributions made it possible for us to continue shipping container loads to the Middle East (each container costing about $6,000).

As a result of the generosity of American citizens from coast to coast, thousands of neglected children have received the clear message: "Someone out there cares about me." Container after container left the Bridgepoint Systems facility, loaded to the hilt with much-needed school supplies, medical supplies, hygiene kits, shoes, clothes, and toys, bound for the CMOC in Kuwait and on to Iraq and later Afghanistan.

The goal was to give other soldiers the resources they needed to perform small acts of kindness wherever they were serving in hopes of winning the hearts and minds of the people.

Toys continue to pour in for Operation Give. These were collected by children at an elementary school.

* * *

With the counterfeiters released from prison soon after their capture, the two captains' lives were in imminent danger. Word soon came from Captain Emad that the counterfeiters had been seen around his house and had obviously discovered who had taken part in the initial raid and their subsequent imprisonment. Fearing for their lives and feeling helpless to protect them, all I could do outside of constantly praying was to stay in touch through email and periodic phone calls.

Having received several death threats, the pilots began moving about the city in secret and changing their daily routines, so as not to be too easy of a target. I spoke with them often, expressing my concern and deep-rooted love for them. They continued to work with my replacements in the CPA, but no one was able to offer any solid protection for them and their families.

Regardless of the threats and dangerous nature of the work, they both continued to assist Dr. Eaman and Hazim any way they could, taking part with her on several trips to orphanages and hospitals. Bonded like brothers and with one heart and mind, we worked as a team promoting the mission of Operation Give.

One day, not long after my departure, I received the sad news that Captain Qies's son had been killed in an attack that was likely meant to kill Captain Qies. Later, I learned that Qies's sister was also killed. Out of desperation and constant fear for their families, the two pilots decided to flee Iraq; Captain Emad took his family to Syria, and Captain Qies headed with his to Egypt. As refugees, they left their homeland in hopes of at least preserving their lives.

With blind courage and balls of steel, Hazim continued to work with my military replacements at the CPA, providing valuable intel regarding insurgent activities in Baghdad. Hazim was fearless, almost to a fault. My concerns centered on his family's well being. I knew that the insurgents would not hesitate to kill all of them at the drop of a hat.

Years later, I received an urgent email from Maha, Hazim's oldest daughter. It seems the Baghdad police, working in conjunction with the insurgents and knowing of his dealings with the US military, set a trap to capture Hazim. Under false charges, he was arrested and thrown into prison, where he remains to this day. My heart aches for his family, who are now fatherless and forced to fend for themselves, barely surviving off of the oldest son's income as a taxi driver. Without going into too much detail, I have exhausted all my efforts, using all of my contacts at the US Embassy in Baghdad to arrange for his release, but to no avail. My heart aches for him and his family's plight.

Finally on my life's destined path and armed with a firm conviction to continue the cause of Operation Give, I was filled with an immovable faith that the Lord would pave the way ahead. Regardless of the hurdles and obstacles in my way, I knew Operation Give would live on, and I have been right.

Within days of my return from Iraq, people from churches, schools, organizations, and the like began calling to see if I would speak to their group about my experiences in Iraq. With my wife by my side, supporting me every step of the way, I began speaking about my miraculous journey in Iraq. Full of passion and love for the Iraqi people, I shared my life-altering experiences in hopes of now winning the hearts and minds of the American people. I wanted everyone to know the untold side to the story, the one the media failed to report, the positive, more humanistic side.

Over and over again, hundreds of times I retold the emotional story of the little crying Iraqi girl I gave a stuffed monkey to, the kind with the long arms and Velcro hands. With tears in my eyes and in all humility, I told of my encounters with the children of Iraq and my efforts to share joy with toys. And the American people got it.

In front of several hundred beautiful children at an elementary school in Stansbury Park, Utah, I told my story of the Iraqi children I had encountered on the streets, in the hospitals, in orphanages, and in poor neighborhoods of Iraq. Prior to my arriving at the school, over the previous week, all the students had brought in their favorite stuffed animals to donate to Operation Give. With thousands of stuffed animals all piled up on the stage, I heard story after story from the teachers of how caring and giving the children had been in donating their prized stuffed animals. A picture was taken of me atop a pile of a thousand stuffed animals that really captures the moment in my memory banks.

After having national news teams in Iraq follow me around and after the President saved my bacon with a few nice words spoken during his 2004 National Prayer Breakfast speech, I had gained a bit of notoriety. This played out well in my favor, as radio talk shows (like The Doug Wright program on KSL in Salt Lake City) and TV shows alike we anxious to interview me in their studios or came down to the warehouse to film our activities. With a little bit of prodding by tenacious Elaine and a few nicely worded press releases, it wasn't hard to get the news crews out for each launching of yet another forty-foot container.

Perhaps in response to my numerous radio and TV interviews, Boy Scouts began calling to inquire about what they might do for their Eagle Scout projects to help Operation Give. With the sky as the limit, Scouts from all over the United States began coming up with the most fantastic ways to help support one of our many projects. From school supplies to soccer balls to shoes, the Scouts came up with the greatest ideas to collect much-needed items. Even my son Matthew, for his Eagle Scout Project, arranged with the janitors of several high schools at the end of the school year to gather up all the items left in lockers for Operation Give. Several truckloads later, my son Matthew donated hundreds of pounds of school supplies for deprived Iraqi children.

With Chief Wiggles as my nickname and a warehouse full of the best toys, all donated for the kids in the Middle East, our "Sharing Joys with Toys" campaign took off as hundreds and hundreds of boxes continued to flow in. But it just wasn't toys being delivered daily by the FedEx truck. As word spread of Operation Give, so did our size and scope as Operation Clean Teeth and Operation Back to School and Operation Play Soccer sprang up. With an annual budget for free domestic shipping from FedEx, people all over the country began sending in toothbrushes and toothpaste, personal hygiene items, school supplies, soccer balls and gear, medical supplies, and everything else imaginable.

Hundreds and hundreds of pallets stacked six feet high with boxes and boxes of donated items filled the warehouse space at Bridgepoint Systems. So many pallets crowded the space that at one point they had to move us to another, larger warehouse just to accommodate the sheer number of boxes being delivered on a daily basis by FedEx. With a pallet jack, a forklift, and a roll of shrink-wrap, each day my son Michael and my brother-in-law Juno sorted, stacked, and wrapped the pallets to prepare them for shipping.

With the help and kindness of attorney Matt Evans, who on his own drew up the paperwork, Operation Give became a legitimate 501c3 not-for-profit organization. As you might recall, Matt also generously provided warehouse space back east that acted as a collection point early on for Operation Give. He was extremely instrumental in setting up Operation Give in the early stages of its development.

Support for the troops in Iraq and Afghanistan continued to grow, as good Americans everywhere, from all walks of life, contributed to the cause any way they could.

OPERATION CHRISTMAS STOCKING

In the fall of 2005, as I was thinking back over the past couple of years, I remembered receiving a large Christmas box from my FedEx friends Gary Becker and Terry DeMuyt. It was a box like nothing I had ever received—a complete Christmas in a box, full of Christmas stockings, presents for everyone in the office, and a Christmas tree with all the ornaments and lights, which transformed our office in the Green Zone into a Christmas wonderland. I will never forget the feeling of complete joy that came over me when I opened the box. Recalling that cherished feeling, I couldn't help but contemplate the joy I could spread to all the troops, away from home during Christmas, if I could just reenact that moment for them.

With the help of Elaine, we launched Operation Christmas Stocking with the goal of sending stuffed Christmas stockings, full of the greatest Christmas treats and goodies, to as many soldiers as possible. Using TV and radio stations, our website, my blog, and any other means we could think of, we spread the word about Operation Christmas Stocking. The word spread like wildfire all over the country, and before I knew it, boxes full of stockings began arriving via FedEx.

Stockings of all shapes and sizes, stuffed full of the most remarkable items, started flooding the warehouse. Through the love and kindness of the American people, that first year we gathered up over twenty thousand Christmas stockings, which were all later sent to our men and women serving in the military, away from home and loved ones, all in some far-off land during the holidays. There was great joy in knowing we were able to share a bit of Christmas from home with so many soldiers.

SPEAKING AT GIRLS' CAMP ATOP THE ROCKY MOUNTAINS

Back and forth, zigging and zagging up the narrow mountain road, I made my way one afternoon to a Girls' Camp up atop one of Utah's beautiful Rocky Mountains. As I exited my car, I could see that a group of young ladies had already started forming in the outdoor amphitheater. With some trepidation, I stood before some one hundred teenage girls, all taking part in a week-long outdoor Girls' Camp. Not totally sure of how I would reach my audience and with nothing more than a prayer in my heart, I started with the story of the young Iraqi girl who I gave a stuffed monkey to. For the next hour, I spoke of the miraculous nature of my journey through Iraq and repeatedly expressed my love for the people of Iraq. Enthralled and somewhat spellbound by my stories of giving, the campers were all touched that day by the spirit of a higher power. Surrounded by God's creations atop a mountain, speaking to a group of young ladies, it was the perfect setting for what became a very memorable experience. Through the feeling in my heart and through the eyes of the girls I spoke to, I knew the work I had been about in Iraq was one I was destined to fulfill.

Full of desire to spread the human side of the war in Iraq, I never declined an opportunity to speak to groups young and old, large and small. Each and every opportunity was special in its own way, especially memorable radio interviews with Doug Wright and Rebecca Cressman. They were so supportive and so eager to help spread the word for the cause of Operation Give. Those two radio talk show hosts understood what it was really all about.

One day, I heard the news that a tsunami had hit Sri Lanka, an island off the southern coast of India. Within days, unbeknownst even to me, a contact was made with an organization on the ground attempting to care for the thousands of displaced people. Shortly after, four forty-foot ocean container loads full of blankets, medical supplies, clothes, and hygiene kits were shipped to that small nation. Then came Katrina and later Tonga and on and on, and the spirit of Operation Give spread and touched the lives of both those who received the much-needed supplies and those who donated the items.

Hearing of my work with Operation Give, the local chapter of the Knights Templar came knocking to see if I wouldn't join up with like-minded individuals in their organization to create a certain amount of humanitarian synergy. Dan Stewart was the first Templar to jump on board with his whole heart and soul, joining forces with my small band of volunteers to attempt to fulfill the mission of Operation Give. He continually volunteered to participate in all of our activities throughout the community, as we attended Boy Scout events, fairs and expos, church and civic gatherings, and, more important, freedom rallies in support of our troops.

Later, in what has become the norm for me with Operation Give, as part of a constant string of miraculous events, I was fortunate enough to hook up with the local chapter of the American Legion. They have been incredible to work with. But even more miraculous and wonderful, Elaine and I both had the good fortune of partnering up with RoseAnn Gunther, who is really an angel from heaven, full of the most Christlike spirit of anyone I have ever met. She has become the third member of our triangle, irreplaceable and priceless.

Since our first days after my return in 2004, due to a string of occurrences and events, we have been forced to move our operations from one warehouse to another. But miraculously, each time without exception, we have been able to find good-hearted people willing to provide us warehouse space for free to receive and store our huge supply of boxes. Finally, as only Elaine can do, she found us a permanent location with Mesa Systems in Salt Lake City, Utah. Mesa Systems has been a gift from God and the most incredible partner we could have ever asked for.

Everything changed in my life as a result of my deployment to Iraq and the subsequent establishment of Operation Give.

* * *

For us in the military, we were there in a war zone—serving our country, fighting and dying for the Iraqi people, but yet we found a place in our hearts to give of ourselves and love the Iraqi people. The bloody Iraqi news stories and all the negative press surrounding our military presence there have vanished from the front pages several years ago.

Yes, the liberation of Iraq and freedom for the Iraqi people came at great cost to the US and to the men and women in the military who have served there. But, there is more to the story then the news would have you believe. You see, a strange phenomenon occurred, as collateral kindness won the hearts and minds of the Iraqi people. There is hope and they do have a chance.

Did you know that the average Iraqi greatly appreciates the sacrifices we have made and all the good that has been done to help make their country safer and to give all of them a new free start, with hope for a brighter future? Did you know that the majority of Iraqis are wonderful, loving, hospitable people?

There is a personal side to the war in Iraq, not depicted in other stories coming out of that region. We the US military were successful in breaking through language and cultural barriers with the Iraqi people and accomplished so much good that has never been reported. I should know—I was there and have witnessed first hand the great amount of good that has been done by thousands and thousands of US soldiers. Through our efforts, thousands of schools have been renovated and remodeled, hundreds and hundreds of miles of roads have been built, repaired and paved, clinics opened, hospitals rebuilt an, small and large businesses started, water and sewage treatment plants built, infrastructure established, a Iraqi style democratic government set up, and the list goes on and on.

The mission of Operation Give is to bring hope and solutions to the deprived and disconnected people of the world, in many cases where the US military operates. We will provide the material supplies and resources to the US Military men and women so they in turn can distribute these items to the people they come in contact with in an effort to ease their suffering and provide them with a brighter future. And that is what we are doing now in many countries around the world, as the work goes on, almost on its own, as the Lord's hand paves the way ahead.

For many years you were fed a daily diet of depressing stories by our fellow citizens in the media, constantly dwelling on the negative and on what has gone wrong in Iraq. Rarely have you ever heard any stories about all the good we have accomplished during those years in Iraq. My question to everyone is why not.

With the ongoing work of Operation Give, I have begun the next phase of my journey. My current stage is only a temporary lay-over, not an end or an arrival, as the next destination on my path was just around the corner when I went back to Iraq for another year in June 2010. I look forward to contributing to the shared future we at Operation Give all enjoy, and I look forward to the additional magical events farther down the road, as I experience the joy that comes with being involved and engaged in an abundant life of giving.

When I went to Iraq, I was committed to give my all. Give my strength—every ounce I could muster. Give my time—every waking hour. Give my talents—everything I had to give. I knew there was a chance I would even have to give my life. But as I returned to American soil, I looked back and realized I had given more than I thought I would. I had given my heart.

This is Chief Wiggles, trying to "do it the Wiggles Way."

OPERATION GIVE TODAY:

The Operation Give Foundation was established and registered in Salt Lake City, Utah, in November 2004. There is still a small group of volunteers in Salt Lake City, Utah (which includes of course Chief Wiggles's wife—Keeyeon—and children, Steve and Elaine Ward and RoseAnn Gunther), and of course Dr. Eaman and others in Iraq, and both military personnel and local nationals in various other countries, who continue to assist in making it possible for us to fulfill the mission of Operation Give. People helping people, to share what we have with people in need—breaking down barriers and changing hearts and helping to create a new reality throughout the world.

Thanks to FedEx, people from all over the US are able to ship their kind donations to our warehouse space at Mesa Systems. Due to the kindness of the owners and managers of Mesa Systems, we are able to do so much that would otherwise be impossible. Donated supplies continue to be distributed to children and now adults too in schools, hospitals, clinics, poor neighborhoods and orphanages, to people in poor conditions and to US soldiers who are attempting to make a difference in their own way wherever they are serving.

Operation Give arose from the needs of children all over Iraq for toys, school supplies, hygiene items, clothing, shoes, and so on, and to provide the soldiers, assisting to rebuild Iraq, the necessary resources and supplies to help bring hope for a new beginning to the children of war-torn countries anywhere. The continued response from individuals and groups reading about Operation Give on the websites is nothing short of remarkable. However, the need is just as great to continue and expand the reach of Operation Give, and to take it from its current state of a "spare time" charity to something much greater.

We have currently shipped over 150 forty-foot ocean container loads to over seventeen countries and are currently shipping fantastic-donated supplies to South Korea where I am working with a number of organizations and orphanages, who are providing care for disabled or handicapped children. I am currently working on a project to set up a small blanket-making factory for the disabled to work in; providing them a job, an income and more importantly a skill.

RoseAnn Gunther still has a group of about fifty women who get together every Wednesday at a church in American Fork, Utah, to quilt, knit, and sew blankets, newborn baby clothes, and a variety of other things for Operation Give to ship around the world.

All of us at Operation Give welcome your involvement and participation and would love to work with you individually or with your church or civic group. Anyone can ship much-needed humanitarian supplies you collect, buy, or make to our warehouse space at Mesa System through FedEx. All you have to do is call or email us to get all the instructions. And don't forget we can help your sons do an Eagle Scout project too.

ABOUT THE AUTHOR

Paul Holton, better known as "Chief Wiggles," is the founder of Operation Give, a humanitarian organization that ships toys, medical supplies, clothes, shoes, sports gear and equipment and educational supplies to children in war-torn and devastated nations throughout the world.

Many became acquainted with Chief Wiggles through his detailed and inspiring wartime blog on the Internet, still actively blogging today at www.chiefwiggles.com. As a chief warrant officer CW5 in the Utah Army National Guard with forty-two years of service, he has served as an interrogator, a debriefer, a HUMINTer, and a Korean linguist. He has been to South Korea more than fifty times, functioning as an interrogation team chief, interpreter, or debriefer of North Korean defectors. For the past year he has been serving the military in Seoul, South Korea, in civil affairs for Eighth Army.

Holton was sent to the Middle East in 1991 during Operation Desert Storm, where he interrogated dozens of Iraqis. *Collateral Kindness* recounts his experiences in Iraq during Operation Iraqi Freedom from 2003 to 2004, from the start of the war through the capture of Saddam Hussein. From June 2010 to June 2011, Holton went back to Iraq on his third deployment and had yet again another amazing magical journey.

Paul has worked for FedEx for the past twenty-two years and was most recently a worldwide account manager. He has taught supply chain management and operation management at the University of Utah and Brigham Young University. He is married to his lovely wife, Keeyeon, and they have four wonderful children and two granddaughters.

WE WOULD LOVE TO HEAR FROM YOU:

www.operationgive.org

www.chiefwiggles.com

www.collateralkindness.com